Familiar Flowers
of
Field & Garden

IN THE FIELDS.

Familiar Flowers
of
Field & Garden

F. Schuyler Mathews

Dover Publications, Inc.
Mineola, New York

Bibliographical Note

This Dover edition, first published in 2020, is an unabridged republication of the work originally printed by D. Appleton and Company, New York, in 1895.

Library of Congress Cataloging-in-Publication Data

Names: Mathews, F. Schuyler (Ferdinand Schuyler), 1854–1938, author.
Title: Familiar flowers of field & garden / F. Schuyler Mathews.
Other titles: Familiar flowers of field and garden
Description: Dover edition. | Mineola, New York : Dover Publications, Inc., 2020. | "This Dover edition, first published in 2020, is an unabridged republication of the work originally printed by D. Appleton and Company, New York, in 1895."
Identifiers: LCCN 2019018317| ISBN 9780486838014 | ISBN 0486838013
Subjects: LCSH: Botany—United States. | Flowers—United States.
Classification: LCC QK118 .M4 2020 | DDC 582.130973—dc23
LC record available at https://lccn.loc.gov/2019018317

Manufactured in the United States by LSC Communications
83801301
www.doverpublications.com

2 4 6 8 10 9 7 5 3 1

2020

INTRODUCTION.

FAMILIARITY with a flower does not always include a knowledge of its name and family. This little volume is intended properly to introduce many familiar characters. We are better pleased to know the golden-rod, virgin's bower, and blood-root by their titled names—*Arguta Solidago*, *Clematis of Virginia*, and *Sanguinaria of Canada*. But the book goes a step further and supplements the introduction with a little friendly gossip based on personal experience. Alas! personal experiences are all more or less different, so I must be pardoned for occasionally appearing to disagree with those whose wide experience, profound research, and scientific training entitle them to acceptation as unquestionable and final authorities. But opportunity is often the means whereby one may arrive at truths not always in the possession of the most learned; and the fact that I have seen the Atamasco lily in bloom in May and even earlier inclines me to the belief that the same opportunity was not afforded to Dr. Asa Gray. *Aster ericoides* I do not find confined to *southern* New England; it is common in northern New Hampshire. It is also the fact that certain variations in type are unrecorded in botanical books to which I have referred; such variations appear in a few of my drawings. The environment of a flower and the length of time in which it blooms are also recorded here with some variation from that according to Dr. Gray. In such instances I have relied upon my own personal experience. Regarding the colors of flowers, I take the liberty of saying that no authority has appeared to be perfectly satisfactory from my particular point of view, and I regret to add that certain records in Dr. Gray's books seem to point to the fact that he was at least partially color-blind.

To any artist who is a colorist it is almost inconceivable that crimson should not be distinguished from scarlet. When it is possible for him to produce fifty distinct variations of red between these two colors, it will be easily understood why he should look on the color-blind person as an eighth wonder of the world!

Color terms are best considered as relative to each other—for instance, blue-violet, violet, violet-purple, purple, purple-magenta, magenta, magenta-red, etc. The name rose-purple is quite indefinite. I suppose it means *pink*-purple; but pink-purple is anomalous. It is a combination of a tint and a hue, and should read either pink-lilac, as a tint, or magenta-purple, as a hue. Now, as these colors are entirely dissimilar, I am left in complete doubt as to which one the botanist refers in using the term rose-purple.

The color of a flower is an important factor in its identification, and I have exercised great care in the selection of an adequate name for it; at the same time, a few popular color-names have been retained when these seemed to be sufficiently near the truth, although certainly not exact. But flowers vary in the presentation of a certain hue; two specimens of *Lilium Philadelphicum* are likely to show two distinct tones of red. Magenta-pink, crimson-pink, and pure pink are varieties of pink common in the Orchis family. *Habenaria fimbriata* is apt to vary from a tint to a light hue. *Cypripedium acaule* is also a variable crimson-pink flower.

By constant reference to Dr. Gray I mean to draw attention to him as our highest botanical authority. The *Manual* and *Field, Forest, and Garden Botany* furnish a scientific background, so to speak, for this volume. A late revision of the Manual furnishes a full, detailed description of certain wild flowers; but a later revision, by Prof. L. H. Bailey, of Field, Forest, and Garden Botany, recently published, will undoubtedly prove the more useful book of the two for those who are inexperienced in botanical research. In Prof. Meehan's Flowers and Ferns of the United States I have found a valuable authority on the habits and characters of our more Western flowers, and Prof. Goodale in his Wild Flowers of America has supplied me with many interesting facts connected with some of our common Eastern flowers. This selection of familiar wild and garden flowers includes those which have seemed most familiar or interesting or even homely to one who spends a great deal of time in the garden and fields surrounding a hillside studio. Most of the Western and Southwestern wild flowers (now in cultivation) grow in this garden, and these, with others of the woods and fields near by, were sketched on the spot. Still other specimens (many of which grew in the Arnold Arboretum near Boston) of various localities were likewise drawn directly from Nature.

What the character of the message is which a wild flower brings to the observant lover of Nature depends largely upon disposition of the individual. This one is susceptible to *no* suggestion; that one sees a vision of the beautiful beyond the conception of the unimaginative; another hears the music of Nature and sees the beautiful as well. Let us hope that there are few Americans of whom Wordsworth might say:

> " A primrose by a river's brim
> A yellow primrose was to him,
> And it was nothing more."

But, on the other hand, who of us can truly say—

> " To me the meanest flower that blows can give
> Thoughts that do often lie too deep for tears"?

There is no doubt in my mind as to what Beethoven was thinking of when he wrote the lovely *scherzo* of his Heroic Symphony. The music is brimful of the woods and fields of springtime. We do not know exactly what Chopin imagined when he composed his Impromptu Fantasia, but its exuberant music suggests the joy and freedom of the birds and flowers in the woods and meadows of June.

A little more familiarity with Nature will lead us to a better understanding of her message—a message she surely has for every one who will but listen.

F. SCHUYLER MATHEWS.

EL FUREIDIS, BLAIR, CAMPTON, N. H.,
October, 1894.

FAMILIAR FLOWERS
OF FIELD AND GARDEN.

CHAPTER I.

MARCH AND APRIL.
Arbutus to Spring Everlasting.

Trailing Arbutus, or Mayflower. *Epigæa repens.* AMONG the favorite flowers of spring, the Pilgrim's Mayflower seems to hold the first place in the heart of a loyal New-Englander. It has even been suggested as a national flower for our country. But the trailing arbutus is too local to stir the enthusiastic interest of our Western and Southern fellow-countrymen; and not long ago, when the subject of a national flower was agitated, a most decided preference was expressed by vote for the golden-rod.

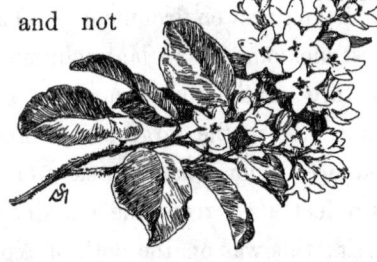

Trailing Arbutus.

However, the sweetness and quiet beauty of the trailing arbutus deserve the highest consideration, and it is at least the representative New England wild flower. The Englishman does not need to ask us, "Where are your fragrant flowers?" John Burroughs says: "Let him look closer and penetrate our forests and visit our ponds and lakes. . . . Let him compare our matchless, rosy-lipped, honey-hearted, trailing arbutus with his own ugly ground ivy (*Nepeta Glechoma*)." We can make our own comparison if we choose, for the ground ivy has become naturalized here, and it may be found in shady places creeping and spreading over the waysides; its flowers are light blue and its leaves kidney-shaped; it can be seen in Prospect Park, Brooklyn, in May. But the ground ivy is not to be mentioned in the same breath with our sweet Mayflower. We must pass what the poet Whittier has to say about it for lack of space, and turn our attention to its natural environment. I have found the loveliest blossoms not in Massachusetts, but in a hilly, wet pasture on the southern slopes of the White Mountains. Here the largest and pinkest blossoms were gathered among damp moss and withered leaves not two feet away from the remains of a winter's snowdrift; this was on the 25th of April. It must be remembered that snowdrifts frequently remain on the southern gorges of the White Hills as late as the middle of May. But the arbutus does not mind the cool breath of a tardy New England spring; on the contrary, it thrives best not in sunny pastures where the sun is doing its warmest work, but in the chill and shadowy retreats of little dells, and in hollows between rocks and groups of stunted firs, where the hillside is wet and cold with patches of melting ice and snow. The starry blossoms are ineffably sweet, and have a frosty, waxy look, and a dainty pink at the edge of the petals, more attractive than the delicate coloring of many a highly prized garden flower. The fresh petals have a taste not unlike muscatel grapes. The flower grows plentifully on the southeastern coast of Massachusetts, and is annually seen for sale in the streets of Boston.

Snowdrop.

Snowdrop.
Galanthus nivalis.

If we call the Mayflower the representative wild flower of New England, then the snowdrop may be called the representative spring flower of Old England! It is not as familiar an object in our own meadow borders as we would wish; yet it grows easily, and thrives in the bleak air of a New England spring. There are several old houses

4 FAMILIAR FLOWERS OF FIELD AND GARDEN.

in Roxbury whose front yards are brightened by this seemingly pathetic, drooping little flower as early as the frost will permit it to appear. It is amazing to see the courageous little thing hanging its dainty head over patches of ice and snow which linger into the middle of March! When the snow and the flower are seen thus together, we are startled by the incongruity of the situation: death and life side by side on the dawn of the *living* year. The 1st of January, New-Year's day, is but a name; the real birthday of the year is marked by the first snowdrop which lifts its head above the winter's snow.

The flower is full of interest, and even under the glass it reveals a new beauty; its inner divisions are short and notched at the end, and are tipped with green; the coloring inside is extremely delicate. The snowdrop belongs to the Amaryllis family.

Scilla, or Squill.

Scilla, or Squill.
Scilla Siberica, or amœna.

The pretty blue scilla, which appears in the grassy plots of our parks and gardens in early spring, is a welcome visitor from Siberia, come to stay in our country. It is perfectly hardy, and its refreshing blue in among the new grass blades is peculiarly harmonious with the background of green. We have one native variety called *S. Fraseri*, or wild hyacinth; this is common on moist banks and prairies from Ohio westward; it grows about ten inches high, and its flowers are pale violet-blue, a color not so pretty as the purer blue of the cultivated Siberian variety, which may be seen in early spring dotting the greensward of the Public Garden, Boston. The bulb of *S. Maritima*, a Mediterranean variety, is officinal, and Sirup of Squills is used for bronchial troubles.

Skunk Cabbage.
Symplocarpus fœtidus.

The earliest harbinger of the spring is the skunk cabbage. This most suggestively repellent plant is about as attractive in odor as it is in name! Yet, aside from this

Skunk Cabbage.

little misfortune, Nature has given the odoriferous cabbage a very *interesting* though not a beautiful appearance, and its very peculiarity invites attention. There is something startling in the fact that the dark, livid-colored thing is related to the spotless calla (what a contrast!), and to the sturdy and happy-looking Jack-in-the-pulpit! But the appearance of the brown-purple spathe must be attractive to animated Nature, otherwise it would not contain so many relics of "a ball that is over." Many insects must have led quite a lively dance inside the spathe, for when we look within its folds we see plenty of remains—honeybees, small flies, bugs, spiders, beetles, and the like. Somehow, I never see a skunk cabbage, with its company of buzzing insects, without thinking of Tam o' Shanter: the little witches are having "a high old time" within, and one can not help feeling somewhat ungracious over the knowledge that beautiful Nature *does* show herself disgusting once in a while; why, in the name of all that is sweet, do dainty honeybees want to visit such a malodorous character? Thoreau says, "Lucky that this flower does not flavor their honey."

Marsh Marigold.
Caltha palustris.

The marsh marigold is another flower which is found for sale in the streets of Boston in spring. It seems a pity that wrong names should attach themselves to our wild flowers, and occasion some confusion regarding their family relations. This flower is not related

Marsh Marigold.

either to the garden calendula (pot marigold) or to the English cowslip; yet it often goes by the latter name (without the English). The flower rather dis-

8 FAMILIAR FLOWERS OF FIELD AND GARDEN.

tantly reminds one of the buttercup, to which it is related; but it is thick and stocky-looking, and deserves some interest on its own account. It will be found in early April beside the brooks as they wind through the meadows, and in springy ground. It is common also in Italy, where we would hardly look for it. The calyx is golden yellow in hue, and the dark-green, thickish leaf is like a rounded kidney in shape.

Hepatica.

Liverwort.
Hepatica triloba.
Hepatica triloba is one of the earliest of our spring flowers, and perhaps one of the most beautiful. It is often described as a

blue flower, but I must object to this on the ground that its blue is only a qualifying condition of its purple. Often the blossoms are nearly white, but as a rule they are blue-purple of extraordinarily delicate quality. The leaves come out later than the flowers, and by the end of summer they are strong and thick, dark green in color, and leathery in texture. They remain green all winter. The flower grows on the edge of the wood, and often in sunny pastures; at least this is so in the Eastern States. A distinguishing point in the *Hepatica* is its hairy flower stem. It is not too early to look for it immediately after the snow has disappeared; in fact, it is contemporaneous with the arbutus, whose blossoms one may often gather within a few feet of a lingering snowdrift!

Dog's-Tooth Violet, or Adder's-Tongue.
Erythronium Americanum.

There is no reason why the adder's-tongue should be called a violet; it is really a lily; and so far as the resemblance in shape between the white root of the plant and a dog's tooth is concerned, that is too trifling for serious consideration. There is a snaky look to the prettily mottled leaf, but nothing to remind one of the snake's tongue. I have found this flower growing beside a little brook as it issued from the border of the wood as late as the 10th of May. The blossom is usually russet yellow, and the upright leaves, spotted with a darker color in delicate pencilings, are readily distinguished from the surrounding green. But we may find some specimens without the slightest trace of this mottled color; so we must remember that Nature, frequently eccentric, refuses to follow a rule unless it is connected with some great underlying principle of creation. This dainty little lily grows as cheerfully on the slopes of Mount Washington, at an altitude of over two thousand feet, as it does in some of the wooded dells of Staten Island. It is an early flower, and may be looked for in April.

Dog's-tooth Violet.

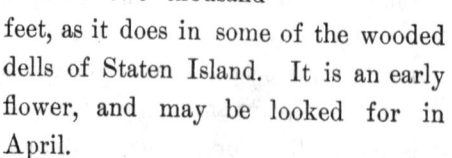

Pansy.
Viola tricolor.

That the pansy is a great favorite in our country is demonstrated by the fact that a seedsman tells me he alone sells over two hundred thousand packages of the seed in a year! The flower is really a large party-colored variety of the violet, and it appears in such variegated colors that it would be difficult to describe even the commonest types. In one strain there are specimens which approach as near to a black flower as it seems possible. I consider the French pansies of M. Bugnot by all odds the finest. But this is a matter of opinion which I am not disposed to urge. Cassier's Odier is a variety of large size and fine color, usually three or five spotted. The pansy should be treated as a biennial; if we wish fine flowers we must raise them from seed each year; they bloom from early spring to midsummer. The Sweet Violet (*V. odorata*), a relation of the pansy, comes from England and Italy, and is not hardy in our gardens of the North. The double-flowered varieties do not seed.

Tulip.
Tulipa Gesneriana.

The tulip comes to us from Asia Minor, but indirectly from Holland. In Arabian ornament, particularly in decorative painting, the flower is frequently represented. Our finest tulips come from Haarlem, Hol-

Tulip.

land, where there are extensive farms devoted to the culture of the splendid flower. In 1634, and three years after, all Holland was crazy over the tulip! This so-called tulipomania was finally ended by State interposition. At one time a collection of fine bulbs of one Wouter Brockholminster sold for $44,100. The first tulip, it is said, came to Europe from Persia, by way of Constantinople, in 1559. The taste for tulips did not reach its height in England until the close of the seventeenth century. The flower ranges without restriction through the chromatic scale, but excepts blue, although it suggests it in the variety named Bleu Celeste. The varieties are simply endless. They flower successively through spring. The tulip is a member of the Lily family.

Blood-root. About the latter end of April, in the
Sanguinaria valley of the Pemigewasset (the river
Canadensis. which gathers its crystal waters from the southern slopes of the Franconia Mountains), beside the road, on the brink of the river, in moist pastures, and beside the woodland brook, may be found the beautiful, broad white flowers of the plant which furnishes a famous specific for coughs and colds. Long before I became acquainted with the plant I had taken many drops of its orange-red blood on lump sugar. It is surprising that in three botanical books I found the juice described as crimson; for

crimson is a blue-red, and this color will not apply in any respect to blood-root. If a bit of the stem of a leaf is squeezed, it will exude an orange-colored juice, which stains everything it comes in contact with. The blood-root leaf grows circling about the rising flower stem, and does not attain its full size of about five inches across until the flower is quite gone. Alas! it goes quickly enough. This is the reason why some of our most beautiful wild flowers are not cultivated by the florists; it does not pay to spend much time over such ephemeral lives. The blood-root is like a butterfly; it comes and goes in a day, like the poppy, to which it is related. The blossom is as lovely and white as a lily, and has a golden center.

Blood-root.

14 FAMILIAR FLOWERS OF FIELD AND GARDEN.

Spring Everlasting.
Antennaria plantaginifolia.

This is an insignificant white, cottony-stemmed plant, which lacks beauty altogether; yet it is so common in the meadows and pastures of the hill country that one must know what it is on account of its conspicuousness in early spring. There are great patches of straggling white seen in the meadows through April, and one wonders, from the distance of a car window in the swiftly passing train, what the "white stuff" is—leastwise, I have been asked such a question. But it is only *Antennaria*, and scarcely merits attention, unless one wishes to examine its peculiar fuzziness through a little microscope.

Æthiopian Calla.
Richardia Africana.

The so-called Calla Lily (it is not a lily, nor a true calla either) is a beautiful, white relative of Jack-in-the-Pulpit. But it is not hardy and must be considered more of a house plant. It comes from Africa, and blooms in spring. The new dwarf variety, Little Gem, is an abundant bloomer.

Spring Everlasting.

CHAPTER II.

APRIL AND MAY.

To Flowering Wintergreen.

Bellwort. The flower of the bellwort is rather
Oakesia sessilifolia. an insignificant, attenuated little
thing, which one would hardly notice unless the plant
was picked, and its hidden side (whence depends the bell) turned into view. The flower is cream-color, the upper surface of the leafage is pale green, and the under surface bluish green. The plant is not often more than eight inches high as it grows in

Seed-pod of the Bellwort.

Bellwort.

16 FAMILIAR FLOWERS OF FIELD AND GARDEN.

Anemone nemorosa.

the White Mountain woods. The green, three-sided seed pod looks like a beechnut. *Uvularia perfoliata* is a very near relation to the flower under consideration, with differences which Prof. Goodale fully explains in his book entitled Wild Flowers of America. It is sufficient here to say that in this variety the stem seems to pass through the base of each one of the leaves. The bellwort flowers in April and May.

Wood Anemone, or Windflower. *Anemone nemorosa.* The wood anemone really belongs in the half-lit woods of spring, when the foliage is undeveloped and its shade is thin and spotty; but I have often found the

Leaf of Anemone nemorosa.

APRIL AND MAY. 17

flower beside the road, and as late, too, as the middle of May. This was among the mountains, where the altitude is apt to retard the advance of spring. The blossom is frail, with five or more white sepals (not petals) sometimes suffused with a delicate crimson pink. The leaves are characteristically wedge-shaped, and on this account there is no excuse for confusing the plant with *Thalictrum anemonoides*, or rue anemone. The leaves of the latter are like those of the meadow rue.

Rue Anemone.
Anemonella thalictroides, or Thalictrum anemonoides.

The dainty rue anemone is often confused with the anemone just described. A glance at my two drawings will at once discover the wide difference between the two little plants. Besides the difference in leafage, *A. nemorosa* is a *one-flowered* plant, while *A. thalictroides* bears quite a cluster of blossoms having six or more white se-

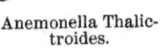

Anemonella Thalictroides.

pals; sometimes these are pinkish. Gray says from five to ten sepals, but the majority of specimens I have gathered seemed to bear six. This flower does not rank as an anemone, and Gray states the reason why; but for me it bears a sufficient and unmistakable family likeness in its leafage to rue or *Thalictrum*. It blooms in May.

Spring Beauty.
Claytonia Virginica.

The little pink spring beauty is a favorite with every one who loves wild flowers. Who would ever suspect it was a kind of pusley? The flower stem, bearing several blossoms, sprawls outward from between two broad, grasslike, dark-green leaves. The flower is delicately veined with a deeper pink, and has five petals and two sepals. Sometimes it is quite white with pink veining. Like a great many other delicate wild flowers, it has a disappointing way of closing as soon as it is picked; but a tumbler of water and sunlight soon work a change in the shy flower, and we need not throw it away as hopelessly withered. I have found the flower on Long Island, and in New Jersey, in April and May. It is quite common in moist places in Prospect Park, Brooklyn.

Dutchman's Breeches.
Dicentra Cucullaria.

The pretty little plant called Dutchman's breeches is common about New York and Brooklyn, and its dainty white flower tipped with yellow may be found in the leaf-mold localities of thin woods, where shade and sunlight are evenly distributed. From its similarity in structure to the familiar Bleeding Heart of the garden (*Dicentra spectabilis*), it will at once show its near relationship with the latter flower. I have never found the Dutchman's breeches in the woods of New Hampshire. It blooms in April and May, and is a low-growing, ornamental-leaved plant of a rather delicate appearance.

Early Saxifrage.
Saxifraga Virginiensis.

The early saxifrage which flowers in April and May is not by any means a conspicuous plant. We will find it nestling among the rocks in the pastures and in shady places beside the wood. The singularly ornamental arrangement of the fresh leaves when the plant is young can not fail to attract notice; they spread around in an even circle like a rosette. But the tiny white flowers are rather insignificant; they are five-pointed, like a star, with a touch of yellow in the center; later on, when the pods appear, they contribute a bit of rich brown to the little plant. Gray says purple, but the color is rather a madder-brown. The name means rock-breaker.

Early Saxifrage.

Large White Trillium.
Trillium grandiflorum.

The large white trillium is considered the finest of all the trilliums; it is certainly a lovely waxy white in color, but inclined toward a pinkish tint as it grows older. It is distinctively a woodland lily, which keeps clear of the moderate sunshine of April. The flower has three long white petals without the marking shown in my drawing of the

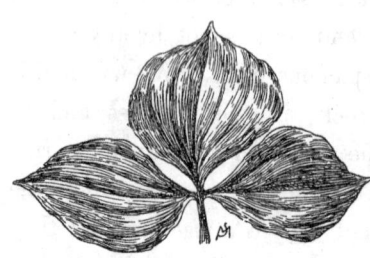

Leaf of large White Trillium.

painted trillium. The leaves are broader than those of the following plant.

Painted Trillium.
Trillium erythrocarpum.

Painted Trillium.

The painted trillium is not as large as the preceding variety, but to my own taste it is more beautiful. The edges of the petals are wavy, and the sharp V-shaped crimson color at the center of the flower is worth a close study under the magnifying glass. It will be noted that Gray says pink; but it is well to remember that he is not always reliable in his color descriptions. The fact is, there are many people who, whether color-blind or not, are incapable of distinguishing subtle variations of color; and the confusion of crimson with pink in the present instance is a demonstration of the fact. The character of the red on the petals of this trillium is crimson—a matter too easily proved by the science of color to admit of any discussion here.

The plant is about eighteen inches high, and the flower is two inches across. Sometimes the leaves show a bluish bloom on the surface, and the stems are stained with a ruddy brown color two thirds of the way down. I have picked handsome specimens beside a woodland road, as late as May 20th, near Campton Village, N. H.; but the flower may be looked for in April, farther south.

Birthroot, or Wake Robin.
Trillium erectum.

Here, again, Gray is rather inaccurate regarding color, for he calls the birthroot dark, dull purple. There is only a trace of purple in the flower. It is dull madder-red in color, sometimes pale, but generally pretty strong. I might explain that brown and purple madder are shades of red approaching maroon in tone, with a greater or less influence of purple. But this by no means guarantees the term purple, any more than the expression "a red face" indicates one of an unqualified scarlet hue. This birthroot is one of those pretty æsthetic red flowers whose color reminds one of certain chrysanthemums. Of the three trilliums mentioned, this seems least attractive; but it is nevertheless a handsome wild flower, which can be proved by arranging it carefully in a vase before one of those black silk Japanese screens which are common in many households. The trilliums are poisonous to taste. I recollect an instance where a would-be young botanist, ignorantly mistaking trillium for Indian turnip, chewed a bit of the root and gave some to the young lady accompanying him in his walk; the consequences were rather serious, and the young people soon had occasion to consult the nearest physician.

Star-Flower.
Trientalis Americana.

The tiny star-flower may be readily found in woods that border the pastures in the hilly country of our Eastern States. It grows in moist places besides the purple violet (*Viola cuculata*) and the foam-flower. Its leaf is not unlike that of the lemon verbena, but it is broader, and grows from the top of a short stem in sets of six and seven, or more, as my drawing accurately represents; it is very shiny and delicate-looking, and of a pale yellow-green color. The perfect, little, starlike flowers are dainty to a fault; they should be studied under a magnifying glass, where their extreme daintiness can be seen to the best advantage. I do not think it is possible to become acquainted with the charming beauty of flower forms and colors without the aid of a botanist's microscope. It is all very well to gather wild flowers for the purpose of becoming acquainted with their family connections and interesting habits, and cast them away when these facts are obtained; but this is something very far short of intimate acquaintance. Only the one who closely observes the frosty, waxy form and color of stamen, pistil, anther, and petal through the mag-

Star-Flower.

nifying glass can know anything of the fairylike beauty which a flower possesses. So this little starflower must be seen under the glass, otherwise it would be passed, as likely as not, for an insignificant character. In Campton it is in its prime about the 10th of May.

Foam-Flower, or False Mitrewort.
Tiarella cordifolia.

The foam-flower grows beside the little star-flower, and blooms about the same time. All through August and September we may find the fuzzy-surfaced, unevenly colored green leaves of the plant, in shape similar to small, narrow maple leaves, growing thickly on the forest floor near some babbling brook. Years ago, when a boy, the symmetrical leaves attracted my eye, and I carried a number of the plants from the White Mountains to my home in Brooklyn, where they were planted in the back yard. Here they flourished fairly well, and I first became acquainted with the fuzzy little blossoms in the following spring. Although there is nothing especially attractive in the flower, it is dainty, and common enough in the

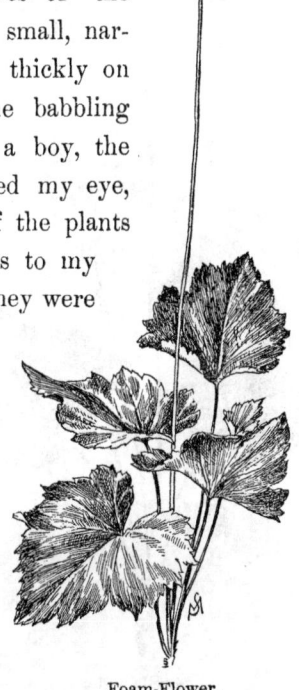

Foam-Flower.

wooded hills of New Hampshire to command our attention. It is nearly related to the true mitrewort, and has a somewhat similar appearance. Its flower stem rises about eight inches above the ground.

Mitrewort, or Bishop's Cap.
Mitella diphylla, and nuda.

The mitrewort, or Bishop's cap, is apt to be found growing beside its false-named relative; and if we are fortunate enough to find the two together, there will be a fine opportunity for comparison, as the flowers are altogether different in construction; this will easily be seen if we patiently examine each under a glass. The starlike blossom of the true mitrewort is fringed in a remarkable manner, reminding one of the conventional rays surrounding the five-pointed figure of a star. The flowers of *M. nuda* grow sparsely on an upright stalk about four or five inches high; they are small and greenish

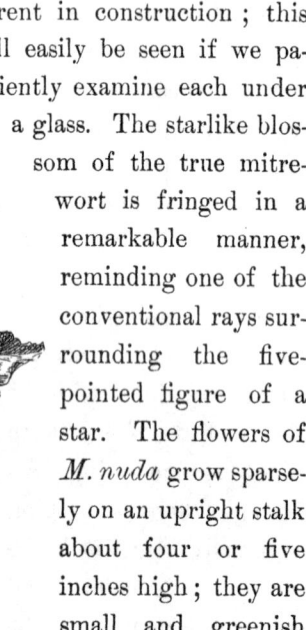

Mitella nuda.

white. *M. diphylla* is a taller plant, bearing a greater number of white flowers. The names for the false and true mitreworts, *Tiarella* and *Mitella*, have a perfectly evident origin; the seed pods look like tiny bishops' mitres. I can hardly agree with Gray, who speaks of the *Tiarella* thus: "Name, diminution of tiara, a turban, not very appropriate." The word tiara for centuries has been applied to a crown, particularly to a bishop's crown, which was cleft from side to side; the Asiatic turban has little to do with the case. The ancient tiara was a round, high cap encompassed by three crowns added by the popes. The King of Persia wore a tiara-shaped crown, adorned with gold and jewels. The word mitre, synonymous with tiara, applies to the pope's triple coronet, the badge of his civic dignity as distinguished from his ecclesiastical rank which the keys represent. With these facts in view, the *Tiarella* is certainly well named. My drawing of the *Mitella nuda* was made from a specimen found in the woods of Vermont in early summer.

White Baneberry.
Actæa alba.

The flower of the white baneberry is fuzzy and white like the foam-flower, but not particularly interesting. It is seen in May. The berries, which appear in late summer, are far more apt to attract notice; they are waxy white, with a purple-black spot, and ovate in shape; the stems which bear the fruit are very thick, and turn red when the berries are fully ripe. The baneberry is a very familiar object in the moist, rich woods of the White Mountains.

Black Snakeroot. I ought not to pass a near relative
Cimicifuga of the white baneberry, called black
racemosa. snakeroot, or bugbane (*Cimicifuga racemosa*). This blooms in summer, and its tall

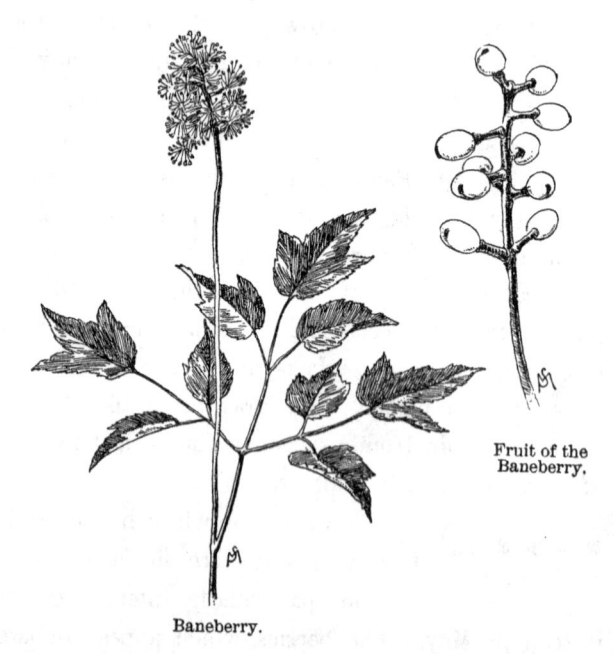

Fruit of the Baneberry.

Baneberry.

spikes of fine white flowers appear better than they smell. The Latin name means, to drive away bugs;

but, strange as it may seem, the plant has become useful in a far better way: it is quite efficacious in driving away neuralgic rheumatism, and doctors prescribe an extract of the root for that purpose.

Wintergreen, or Checkerberry.
Gaultheria procumbens.

Although the wintergreen flowers as late as July, its dark green, roundish leaves and bright scarlet berries are familiar objects in the woods in spring when there is little that is green scattered over the woodland floor to hide the pretty shiny plant from view. The berries grow so plentiful in southeastern Massachusetts that they are picked and brought to Boston, where they may be found for sale in many of the fruit stores. The berries remain on the evergreen plants all winter; in spring they are found in plenty on the foothills of the White Mountains. The flower is tiny and waxlike, and tastes as strongly aromatic as the berry does.

Wintergreen, or Checkerberry.

Flowering Wintergreen, or Fringed Polygala.
Polygala paucifolia.

The flowering wintergreen, a delicate little plant, is no relative of the checkerberry; the latter belongs to the Heath family, and the former to the Polygala family. The flowering wintergreen bears a conspicuous crimson-pink blossom, perhaps three quarters of an inch long, with a fringed crest; the leaves are crowded at the summit of the slender stem, and from among these the pretty flower looks out. The plant is hardly four inches high, and blossoms in May and June; the specimen from which my drawing was made grew on the edge of the Dismal Pool in the Crawford Notch, N. H.

Flowering Wintergreen.

CHAPTER III.

MAY.

Yellow Violet to Pitcher Plant.

Yellow Violet.
Viola pubescens.

THE yellow violet, commonly called the downy yellow violet, grows on the edge of the wood where sunlight and shadow are mixed. I am best acquainted with the smooth variety, which can be found in a certain locality in the Pemigewasset Valley, and is a never-ending source of delight to me in late spring. I know of no other spot for miles north and south where there is more. This particular patch is broad and thick, and about the 10th of May one may gather hundreds of blossoms without moving beyond a space ten yards square. I never found

Downy Yellow Violet.

this flower, as Bryant says, "in forest bare," nor could I ever discover the "faint perfume"; and, although the valleys of the White Mountains hold many a drift of snow as late as May, not a sign of snow is ever seen about the patch I have alluded to. Nor does the little flower seem to bend its "gentle eye" earthward. My drawing certainly tells the exact truth, as it was made on the spot where the violets grew, and was taken from a single specimen. These two little yellow beauties held their heads pretty high—something like ten inches above the ground. But we must not take the poet on any grounds of scientific accuracy; the truth he aims for is spiritual and not material; the last three verses of Bryant's poem are the best ones to judge it by. The yellow of this flower is golden in character, but considerably paler than dandelion yellow, and is veined with brownish purple. The blossom is very small, and springs up from between a pair of leaves which start from a bare stem about eight or nine inches tall.

Purple Violet.
Viola cuculata.

The specimen which I have drawn of the purple violet (commonly called *blue*, but I prefer the truer *purple*) was gathered on the 25th of May, in a very wet spot not more than a hundred yards away from the yellow violet patch just mentioned. It makes a great difference in regard to its personal appearance where a flower happens to grow. This specimen was reared exactly under the most advantageous conditions for a high development; the flower measured over an inch and a quarter in length. We all know that there are plenty of violets to be found sprinkled over hillside and pasture which do not attain even a moderate size; but if one wishes to gather some really fine specimens, they must be sought in cool, shady dells, where the soil is rich and there is plenty of spring water.

Purple Violet.

Bird-foot Violet.
Viola pedata.

The pronounced type of slender leafage belonging to the bird-foot violet is in astonishing contrast with the heart-shaped leaf which we are accustomed to associate with violets; this instance of unlikeness in a flower family is a demonstration of the fact that superficial appearances count for very little in botany,

34 FAMILIAR FLOWERS OF FIELD AND GARDEN.

which often finds among hidden things that which is essential for the establishment of scientific truth.

Bird-foot Violet.

Thus it is that the ovaries and stigma of the rue anemone (*Anemonella thalictroides*), and not the leaf, decide that the flower is not a true anemone. But nothing is more attractively symmetrical in plant form than this particular violet's leaf; pressed flat on a piece of paper, its delicate outline is an interesting study for one who loves the decorative side of Nature.

The flower is rich in blue-purple color, and sometimes the two upper petals are a strong violet-purple. The little touch of orange-yellow in the center is extremely effective. In the sandy soil of Nantucket, and on the borders of Buzzard's Bay, this violet blooms with spendthrift prodigality, its great clumps of light blue-purple bloom decorating the springtime meadows as far as the eye can reach. The blossoms droop sadly after being picked, but revive at once on being placed in a glass of water. I have found the flower in its prime in Nantucket on the 25th of May.

Sweet White Violet. The sweet
Viola blanda. white violet
has the faintest and most delicate perfume imaginable. I should think Bryant had *this* flower in mind when he wrote about the yellow violet, for besides its "faint perfume" it is readily found in the "bare forest." The blossom is tiny, but extremely pretty

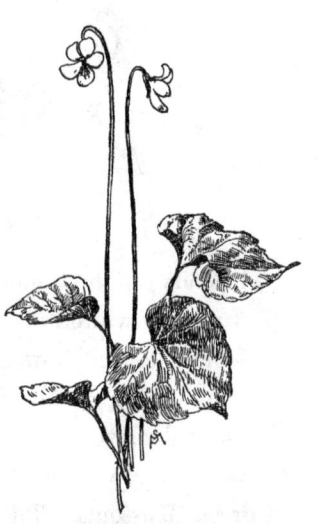

Sweet White Violet.

under the microscope, the lower petal showing purple striping in delicate hair lines. It is very common in the woods of the White Mountains in May.

Solomon's Seal.
Polygonatum biflorum.

Solomon's seal is easily indentified, as it grows beside some woodland road in early May, by its light green leaves, and its long, gracefully curved stalk, from which

Solomon's Seal.

depends on the under side a series of tiny, greenish or creamy-white flowers always arranged in pairs. In September the flowers are replaced by deep violet-blue berries. The charm of Solomon's seal is the graceful curve of its stalk; its flowers are unattractive, and are somewhat similar in form to wintergreen blossoms. The name had its origin in the pitted appearance of the root, which bears a round scar left by the broken-off old stalk; this is so unlike the impression of a seal in shiny red wax that it requires the utmost stretch of imagination to be reconciled to the questionable resemblance.

There is a great deal in pure imagination—more than some of us are willing to take any part in. For instance, who ever saw any resemblance between a "big dipper" and a "big bear"? yet these are both one series of celestial, imaginative outlines which are intimately associated with the north star! But Solomon's seal is a suggestive name, and we should not quarrel with it. As a similarity of outlines is suggestive, however, I would like to draw attention to the fact that the petal of the dog's-tooth violet closely resembles a canine tooth; but, strangely enough, this is not the reason why the flower was so named, as the previous description of it will explain.

Outline of Dog's Tooth.
Outline of Petal of Dog's-Tooth Violet.

False Solomon's Seal.
Smilacina racemosa.

The false Solomon's seal is in my estimation even more beautiful than the true. Its spike of fine white flowers is like the *Spiræa Japonica*; besides, its wavy, bright green leaf with the parallel veining is particularly graceful. Most wild flowers, like the true Solomon's seal, have rather insignificant blossoms; but there is nothing meager about the bloom

Smilacina Racemosa.

of this little plant. It deserves cultivation, and, in truth, if it is transplanted to a position in the garden similar to its natural environment, it will flourish most satisfactorily. It is a shame that any aspersion of falsity should attach to it; why should not a plant so deserving have its own good name? We might as well call a Frenchman a false Englishman! There is such poverty displayed among names that we may find a Bald Knob and Black Mountain in nearly every mountain district of our Atlantic States. It seems as though our nation was lacking in both originality and imagination! The false and the true Solomon's seals will be found growing on the edge of the wood together; but the latter is a trifle earlier in bloom. *S. racemosa* has a pale reddish berry speckled like a bird's egg.

Smilacina stellata. *Smilacina stellata* is another so-called false Solomon's seal, which also deserves a name of its own. It grows not quite as high as *S. racemosa*, and it is not so pretty. I found it thickly spread

Smilacina Stellata.

over the bank of the Pemigewasset River, where it seemed to grow with more luxuriance than it did in the shady pasture near the wood. Its starry flowers are white, and the berries are small and black-purple in color. It is in its prime about the middle of May.

Smilacina trifolia. The variety of false Solomon's seal named *Smilacina trifolia* is about six inches tall and has two larger lower leaves and one smaller upper one, which at their bases sheath the stem; the few flowers which are clustered at the termination of this stem are small and white. The plant grows in cold, wet places, and is common in some parts of the White Hills; it flowers in June or early July.

Maianthemum Canadense, or Smilacina bifolia. *Maianthemum Canadense* is still another but smaller false Solomon's seal. This delicate little character, growing not much over five inches high, fairly carpets the thinner woods where they adjoin the pas-

Maianthemum Canadense.

ture. The leaves are bright green, but the short raceme of flowers is rather insignificant. The flow-

Clintonia Borealis.

ers are in their prime about the latter end of May in the North. The little spike of translucent, reddish berries is seen in the latter end of summer.

Clintonia borealis. *Clintonia borealis* is a pretty little pale straw-yellow lily whose only fault, it seems to me, lies in its weak and uncertain coloring. Sometimes the half-matured flowers look decidedly green, again the full flower appears a deep cream-color. If the horticulturists could only force it into a good white and increase its size, there might be a future before our dainty *Clintonia*. The flower was named for the Governor of New York, for what reason nobody knows. Its green leaf is smooth and shiny, and about the same in shape, color, and character as that of the lily-of-the-valley. Perhaps the color of the mature flower might more exactly be called a pale, dull Naples yellow. The flower is in bloom about the end of May northward, and can be found in moist rich woods. The berries are seen in late August; they are a beautiful Antwerp-blue color.

Jack-in-the-Pulpit, or Indian Turnip. *Arisæma triphyllum.* Jack-in-the-pulpit is a happy-looking flower—if a flower can be said to look happy—and its striped suit reminds one of the conventional, funny circus clown. It is too bad to make such a comparison; but I must let it stand, because there are few other flowers (at least wild flowers) which are so suggest-

MAY. 43

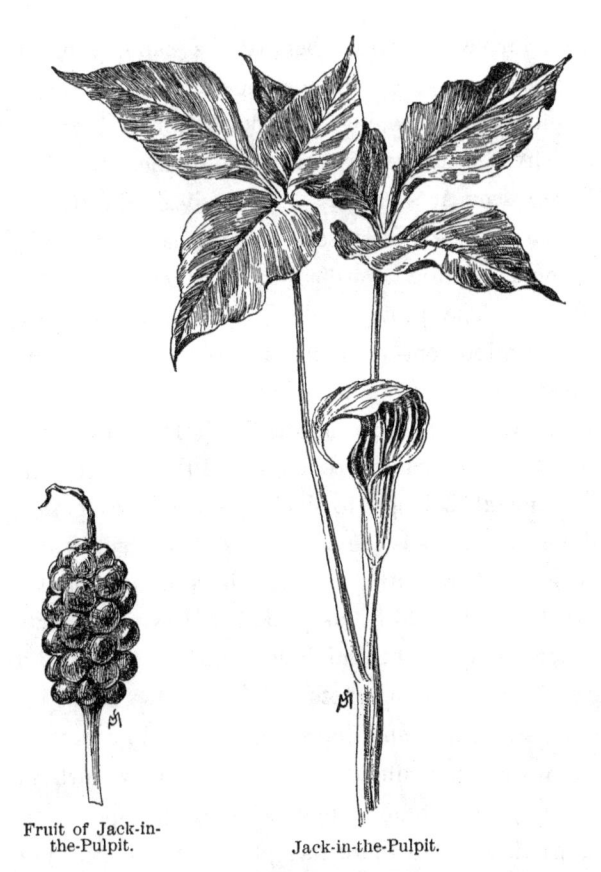

Fruit of Jack-in-
the-Pulpit.   Jack-in-the-Pulpit.

ively humorous. Certainly, the poet who wrote the
verses about Jack in Lilliput Levee found something
delightfully fresh and sprightly in his character.

What is particularly boyish about this plant is
the odd way it hides the prettily striped suit of

brown-purple and white beneath its panoply of six gay green leaves. It reminds one of some little eight-year-old romper peeping out from behind a door, just a bit shy because he has nice clean clothes on. Jack is rarely seen at a careless glance—he is mostly hidden beneath the six leaves—and we have actually to take hold of him in order to investigate his novel clothing. The pretty little brown club inside the spathe reminds one of a miniature Bologna sausage; the way the top of the flower hangs over the cup suggests a wallet with perhaps some gold inside; but that is the pity of it, there is no gold there! All the yellow metal belongs to Jack's cousin, the spotless white calla. This is the only thing about Jack which we can find fault with; he might have pleased us better with a little gold in his pocket. However, in late summer he leaves behind him a cluster of splendid scarlet berries like my sketch.

Some of the plants have pale green flowers with whitish stripes, while others are extremely dark in coloring. I have found a few of the lightest specimens in a pasture where there was plenty of sunlight, but the darkest ones seem to grow beside a wet, springy dell, within a stone's throw of my cottage. It would not seem springtime to me if there was not at least one Jack in a majolica jar in my studio. The plant flowers in May and early June. The root has a sharp,

MAY. 45

stingy taste, without a reminder of turnip about it. There are plenty of Jack-in-the-Pulpits to be found in the vicinity of Silver Lake, Staten Island, or, in fact, almost any wet, shady place.

Pitcher Plant.

Pitcher Plant.   The odd, tubular-shaped leaves of
Sarracenia purpurea.   the pitcher plant deserve close at-

tention. It is said that the decomposed insects which we may find at the bottom of the "pitchers" contribute to the nourishment of the plant. Inside of the leaves there is a sweet secretion which attracts insects; after they crawl in through the mouth, escape is wellnigh impossible, as the hairy sides of the tube impede their flight and render the walking anything but easy. The flowers are oddly colored with green and brownish purple, and come to maturity about the end of May and the beginning of June. The plant is always found in boggy places where the sunshine is partly obscured; and with this environment, it must be admitted, its appearance is rather uncanny.

CHAPTER IV.

MAY AND JUNE.

Robin's Plantain to Cranberry.

Robin's Plantain.
Erigeron bellidifolius.

The robin's plantain is a deceptive-looking character; it is easily mistaken for an aster. The yellow center, the blue-purple rays, and the size and shape of the flowers remind one of the autumn flower which has prematurely come into bloom. Of course, it is a near relative of the aster, but its appearance is marked by a great many differences. It grows about a foot high; sometimes less, sometimes more. The large leaves I have drawn at the foot of the plant frequently lie prone on the ground.

Robin's Plantain.

There is a hairy look to stem and flower, which is not altogether aster-like; the leaves are small and far between, and the stem is thick and juicy. The flowers come about the 1st of June, and are seen in plenty beside the road and in damp places.

Bluets.
Houstonia cærulea.

Of all the dainty, tiny flowers that bloom in late spring, the little bluets is perhaps the daintiest. What is satisfactory, too, about the flower is the fact that it does not shut up and wilt immediately after being picked. It is such an attractive little thing that Mr. W. Atlee Burpee, the horticulturist, has introduced it to the public as a cultivated garden flower. The flower is barely half an inch across; it is a simple-looking, four-rayed corolla, sometimes white, but oftener pale-purplish blue, with a dainty spot of golden yellow around its eye. In Campton the roadsides and meadows are starred all over with little bunches of this dainty gem. From the middle of May to the end of June the flower continues to bloom in sunshine and shadow; in fact, it grows everywhere except in the dark, wild forest. The flower was named for Dr.

Bluets.

MAY AND JUNE. 49

Houston, an English physician, who was interested in the flora of Mexico.

Blue-eyed Grass. I ought to have said blue-eyed grass
Sisyrinchium was the only flower daintier than
Bermudiana. bluets, if one is to speak from his
own point of view; yet this is hardly fair, because the blue-eyed grass is a bolder and larger flower, just reminding one of a violet. Unfortunately, it shuts up at once on being picked, and unless there is plenty of sunlight it refuses to open its eye at all; its color is purplish ultramarine blue, darker toward the center, where there is a touch of pure gold. There is a curious notch in each one of the six divisions of the perianth, from which protrudes a little point, in shape like a thorn. The leaves are narrow, and look like blue Kentucky grass. The flower stands about ten inches high, and is generally shut in the afternoon; sometimes there are three buds on a stalk, but I never found more than one open at a time. The flower grows in clumps on the meadow, in the pasture, and at the edge of the wood, but generally in moist places.

Blue-eyed Grass.

I have transplanted it successfully to the grounds in front of my cottage, where it flourishes and spreads from year to year. It reaches its prime about the 1st of June. It is a relative of the iris.

Yellow Star-grass. Star-grass is a pretty little yellow
Hypoxys erecta. flower with apparently six pointed petals (in reality the six divisions of the perianth), which blooms almost anywhere (in the meadows) in May and June. The flower stem, about six inches tall, terminates in two or three flowers as broad as a nickel, perhaps one in full bloom and two others in bud. The outside of the flower is greenish; the leaves are grasslike and hairy. It belongs to the Amaryllis family, and is closely related to the narcissus.

Common Cinquefoil. The very common cinquefoil is
Potentilla Canadensis. found beside the country highways and by-ways, and in pasture, meadow, and woodland. It is so often mistaken for a yellow-flowered strawberry that I must at once show the difference. Notice in my drawing of the strawberry that the stems of the leaves are hairy; the stems of our cinquefoil are brown and as sharp and clean as a piano wire. Also notice that the cinquefoil has five leaves, or rather divisions of a leaf, and the strawberry has three; the latter little plant never goes beyond a three-divisioned leaf, but

MAY AND JUNE.

devotes all the rest of its strength to strawberries. Furthermore, there is only one yellow-flowered strawberry (*Fragaria Indica*), and this is not very common; I found it once in Staten Island some years ago, and have not seen it since. The common cinquefoil blooms from June to September. But there is a *three*-leaved cinquefoil, and, for the sake of comparison, I have carefully drawn it.

Norway Cinquefoil. The Norway
Potentilla Norvegica. cinquefoil is a tall branching plant with a leaf of three divisions and a very hairy appearance. It has a yellow flower similar to *P. Canadensis;* but, after all, the similarity is slight if my drawings are carefully compared. I found this plant blooming in early August within three feet of my studio window; it did not seem to be in

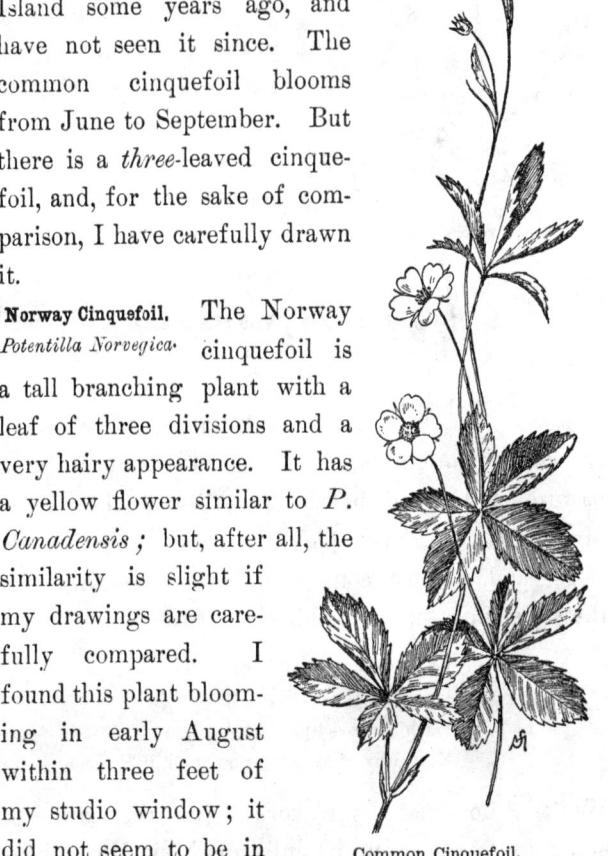

Common Cinquefoil.

52 FAMILIAR FLOWERS OF FIELD AND GARDEN.

any of the fields in the same vicinity. The shrubby cinquefoil (*P. fruticosa*) is common in wet grounds northward, grows about three feet high, and has five to seven leaflets and loose clusters of yellow flowers similar in character to those of the common variety.

Norway Cinquefoil.

Wild Strawberry.
Fragaria Virginiana.

Our wild strawberry is so well known that it scarcely needs mention here. It grows luxuriantly in pasture and wood in the foothills of the White Mountains. I never pick the berries on the hillsides—and, I must confess, fight the mosquitoes at the same time—without thinking of the

> "Barefoot boy, with cheek of tan,
> .   .   .   .   .
> With thy red lip, redder still
> Kissed by strawberries on the hill."

Whittier does not say a word about the bare legs and mosquitoes. In the hills of New Hampshire,

MAY AND JUNE. 53

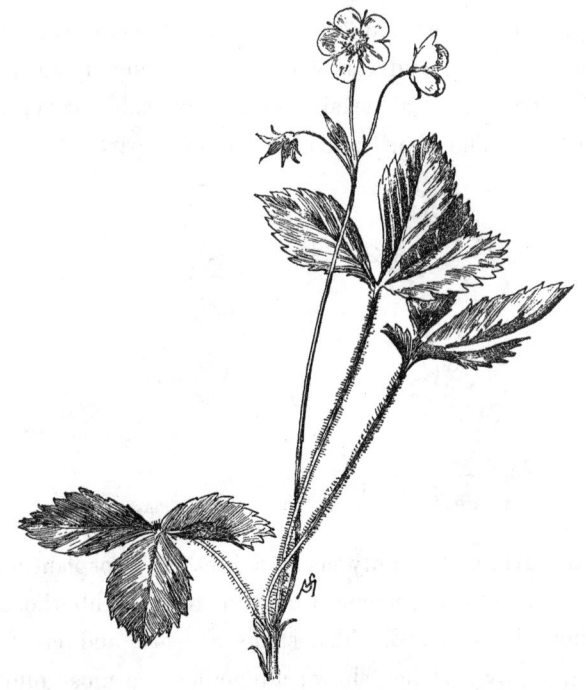

Wild Strawberry.

at least, the mosquito and the wild strawberry are inseparable!

Moss Pink.
Phlox subulata.

The little flower called moss pink is common in some parts of New York and New Jersey, and in the vicinity of Philadelphia in May and early June the hillsides are stained crimson with the pretty flower. I found a thick patch of it in the Pemigewasset Valley, but confined to one locality. It seems certain that it spread and ran wild from a cemetery in the vicinity, where a certain lot is noticeably covered with it. The plant flourishes in some parts of Cen-

Moss Pink.   Moss Pink in Buds.

tral Park, and it only needs a hint of transplanting to run wild over everything in the neighborhood where it is placed. The stems are low and creeping, as my sketches show; altogether the moss pink has a mossy look, and is well named.

Wild Columbine. The scarlet and yellow columbine is
Aquilegia one of our most beautiful wild flow-
Canadensis. ers. It is my experience that certain flowers have favorite haunts which are exclusively held by them year after year, without a shadow of change. There are three spots I know of in the pasture land of Campton where the pretty columbine may always be found; a search for the flower any-

Wild Columbine.

where else for two miles around has always proved useless. Nothing is daintier or more beautiful than the color effect of this graceful blossom among the gray rocks of a hillside pasture. The flower is in its prime about the 1st of June, and is nearly always found beside some lichen-covered rock in the company of young, velvety mullein leaves which have just pushed themselves above ground.

Moccason Flower. *Cypripedium acaule.* The pink moccason flower is another one of those exclusive characters which prefers the limitations of some moist and shady locality; it can not be found, as the violet is, under a variety of conditions. The flower is very handsome; in fact, it does not look like an ordinary wild flower, but rather like an expensive, cultivated orchid. I never found it, as Gray suggests, under evergreens, but among the withered leaves that lie under birch, beech, poplar, and maple. But this is a matter of individual experience which may be added to some other quite different ones; it only points to the fact that Nature is not always regular in her habits. The point of beauty in the flower is its crimson-pink pouch or sac, which is delicately veined with a deeper pink, and its purplish brown and green sepals and petals. The two light-green leaves are parallel-ribbed, but otherwise in appearance are like those of the lily-of-the-valley.

Cypripedium acaule.

58 FAMILIAR FLOWERS OF FIELD AND GARDEN.

The plant flowers in early June. The name *Cypripedium* in English would be Venus's slipper.

Yellow Lady's Slipper.
Cypripedium parviflorum.
The smaller yellow lady's slipper, sister to the flower just described, is found in similar situations where the ground is moist, and has the addition of a slight perfume. The sac is small, and is a deep-toned yellow; the sepals are a sienna brown. Another larger yellow variety (*C. pubescens*), one of our commonest orchids, has a lighter-colored sac, and is without perfume; but I consider the smaller variety more beautiful. The time of flowering for both is early summer.

Cypripedium parviflorum.

MAY AND JUNE.

Snake's Mouth.
Pogonia ophioglossoides.

The snake's mouth is a pretty little orchid of a most delicate pure pink color, which may be found in swampy places if one does not mind getting the feet wet—no swamp, no snake's mouth; that is my experience. The prettily formed little flower has a sweet smell, is about an inch long, or less, and should be examined under a glass. It blooms in June.

Calopogon pulchellus.

The *Calopogon pulchellus* belongs to the same family group (*Orchis*) as the moccason flower, arethusa, and snake's mouth; indeed, the latter is its boon companion; the two are most likely to be found in each other's company. The flower is a beautiful crimson

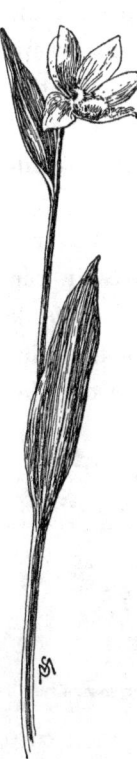

Snake's mouth.

Calopogon pulchellus.

pink, and its lip is bearded with white, yellow, and crimson blunt-tipped hairs; its leaf is narrow and grasslike. It may be found in wet bogs during the early summer. Prof. Goodale says, comparing the moccason flower with the *Calopogon:* "The *labellum* in *Calopogon* appears to be upside down, while that of the moccason flower is properly pendent; but the fact is, it is only by a twist in the ovary, or perhaps in the pedicel, that the latter flower has assumed this position." But unerring Nature does not do anything wrong end up, and both flowers appear standing on their feet!

Purple Azalea, or Pinxter Flower.
Rhododendron nudiflorum.

Late in spring the purple azalea will be found in swampy places in the East, and its lovely crimson-pink color is a charming foil for the pale-green tints of May which the French artist Corot delighted in painting. The wild azalea and the rhododendron are likely to be somewhat confused in our minds, so I must draw attention to some distinguishing differences. The true azaleas have deciduous leaves, and the rhododendrons have evergreen leaves. The azaleas are characterized by a funnel-shaped tube with an irregular edge; there are about five stamens in each tube, while the rhododen-

Purple Azalea.

dron, as a rule, has double that number. The flowers of the azalea appear with or precede the leaves; the rhododendron flowers later, in early summer, and usually grows on the mountain side. Emerson's rhodora (*Rhododendron rhodora*) is a low-growing shrub about two feet high, with hardly any other superficial appearance to distinguish it from *R. nudiflorum*, except it be the superiority of its magenta-pink color, its small corolla which is three-lobed above and two-lipped below, and its shorter stamens. I never was fortunate enough to find either of these varieties in New Hampshire among the hills.

Rhodora.

In Massachusetts both are quite common. The striking resemblance of the rhodora to honeysuckle will be at once perceived; but they are *not* related to each other.

Great Laurel, or Rhododendron.
Rhododendron maximum.

The rhododendron is not so common in our Eastern States; it is far more plentiful among the Alleghany Mountains, where it grows luxuriantly under the softened light of the half-lit woods. It is evidently too cold for the shrub in the woods of the

62 FAMILIAR FLOWERS OF FIELD AND GARDEN.

White Mountains, where the thermometer frequently registers 30° below zero. Gray's description of

Rhododendron (Great Laurel).

the flower is sufficiently simple for any one to understand: "Pale rose, or nearly white corolla, one inch broad, greenish in the throat, on the upper side more or less spotted with yellow or else reddish." But the cultivated flowers bloom (in great clusters) in the Public Garden of Boston, in magenta and pinkish-white tints, and attain a size of over an inch and a half

MAY AND JUNE. 63

in diameter.* The leaves hold their olive-green color all winter. The time of flowering is early summer.

Cranberry, Large.
Vaccinium macrocarpon.

The large cranberry grows in boggy places from New Jersey to Maine, and may be found in bloom in early summer. The berry is ripe in early autumn; the finest one is dark red in color, and comes from the boggy districts of Cape Cod. Nantucket also has its cranberry bogs, and the season of picking is quite an important event for the islanders. The plant is small, the wiry stems usually reaching a length of about eight or nine inches; but sometimes they develop a length of two feet or more. It is curious to find that such totally different-looking plants as the rhododendron and the cranberry are relatives; they belong to the Heath family.

Cranberry.

---

* The cultivated varieties (hybrids), arise generally from *R. Catawbiense, R. Ponticum,* and the tender *R. arboreum* of the Himalayas.

CHAPTER V.

MAY, JUNE, AND JULY.

Rattlesnake-Plantain to Indian Poke.

Rattlesnake-Plantain.
Goodyera pubescens.

THE rattlesnake-plantain is a most interesting character. Its peculiar wavy-edged, dark-green leaves are covered with a network of fine white lines. The flowers are small, white, and waxy-looking, and the leaves are circled below in a rosette figure; they are evergreen. In winter one may find the little plant nestled in some out-of-the-way woodland nook, where it would not so easily be discovered in summer. It flowers in July. Another variety (*G. repens*) is smaller, and flowers in a loose, one-sided spike; this is common in the White Mountains.

Rattlesnake-Plantain.

MAY, JUNE, AND JULY.

Arethusa.
Arethusa bulbosa.

Arethusa is an elusive nymph of whose whereabouts one is never quite certain. As I have searched for and found the flower only within the White Mountain district, it may be without my knowledge a familiar object in other parts of the country. But I know of only two wet, boggy spots where it grows, and half the time I do not succeed in capturing it even in these locations. Certainly it is one of the loveliest of our orchids, and is well worth a tiresome search and inevitably wet feet. The slim stem is about eight inches high, and the pretty crimson-pink flower, in profile, reminds one of a hand with the five fingers held loosely upward. The time of flowering is late spring and early summer, but I have found a specimen as late as the 1st of August.

Arethusa.

Fringed-Orchis.
Habenaria fimbriata.

I should call the flowers of the fringed-orchis magenta pink, though undoubtedly they may present some variations of this hue. It is a very beautiful plant, and consequently attracted the attention and admiration of the eccentric Henry D. Thoreau, who speaks of it as a beauty "who has never strayed beyond the convent bell." His remark, it seems to me, applies rather to *Arethusa*, who is certainly much more of a recluse; but in A Week on the Concord and Merrimac Rivers he says, "Nature seemed to have adorned herself for our departure with a profusion of fringes and curls, mingled with the bright tints of flowers." Now, this orchis is the very perfection of Nature's fringing in bright flower tints, and in my mind Thoreau's words somehow connect themselves with this lovely flower. It blooms in wet meadows in early summer. There are

Fringed Orchis.

three other orchises common in the foothills of the White Mountains—*H. psycodes*, small but sweet-scented magenta flowers; *H. lacera*, homely pale greenish flowers; and *H. virescens*, a spike of dull greenish flowers; these have been found in bloom in more or less wet ground from June 20th to July 24th.

Showy Orchis.
Orchis spectabilis.

The showy orchis, Gray says, is the only *true* orchis we have. It is a pretty flower, the upper part purplish pink, and the lower lip white; there are few blossoms on a stem—not more than three or four. The two leaves are not unlike those of the lily-of-the-valley. The flower seems to me rather rare, as I have found but few specimens in the woods of the White Mountains. It generally grows in rich black soil made up of decayed leaves, and seems to prefer the deep and shady forest. Its time of flowering is May and June.

Showy Orchis.

Golden Senecio, or Ragwort.
Senecio aureus.

The golden senecio, or ragwort, has a delightfully bright color which illumines the meadows where the flower happens to grow with an amber light such as we may see in some of the paintings of the old master, Claude Lorraine. There is something very beautiful in this mixture of golden yellow with the misty-toned green of the meadows in July when the senecio is in full bloom. The flower resembles an aster in form, but the leaves have an individuality of their own; they are also variable in type; perhaps the commonest leaf is heart-shaped. The plant gets its name from its hairy appearance (certain of the species have a cottony look), or from the downy effect of the flower head when it has passed the period of bloom. Thoreau says in his journal, July 2d: "I see the downy heads of the senecio gone to seed, thistlelike, but small. The *Gnaphaliums*" (everlasting flowers) "and this are among the earliest to present this appearance." The word senecio is derived from *senex*, an old man, and

Golden Senecio.

MAY, JUNE, AND JULY. 69

the flower at this period, in my opinion, merits this appropriate name. The plant attains a height of from one to three feet.

Shin-Leaf.
Pyrola elliptica.

The euphonious name shin-leaf was tacked on the pretty *Pyrola* for a reason which one may readily guess; — the leaves were used as a cure for bruises. From the days of my early youth the name "shin-plaster" has been familiar as it must be to every New York boy of some years ago. I remember that my father called court-plaster, or in fact anything of the kind, without discrimination, either shin-plaster or sticking plaster. So the pretty flower suffers by reason of an old custom. The *Pyrola* grows about six inches high, is found in woody dells, or damp, shady byways, and flowers in June and July. Its leaves are olive-green, and the blossoms are greenish white.

Pyrola.

70 FAMILIAR FLOWERS OF FIELD AND GARDEN.

Pipsissewa.
Chimaphila umbellata.

The pipsissewa is a sweet-scented little woodland flower, which is common in all dry, sandy soils. I have found it plentiful in the famous "Pine" district of New Jersey, in Saddle River Valley in the same State, and in the pine woods of New Hampshire. The flowers are waxy and flesh-colored, and the leaves are shiny olive-green; they keep their color even in winter. It flowers in June and July. There is a variety, common in the White Mountains, with white-spotted leaves toothed on the edge like a saw. This is named *C. maculata*. It is interesting to examine the blossoms under a magnifying glass, where the beauty of the frosty pink flower with its purple anthers will prove quite a revelation.

Pipsissewa.

MAY, JUNE, AND JULY.

Yellow Wood-Sorrel.
Oxalis stricta.
The little yellow wood-sorrel is extremely common in meadow, woodland, and pasture, and the tiny clover-like leaf may be recognized anywhere snuggling in the grass from May to October. The flower is rather insignificant, and of a pale buttercup yellow.

White Wood-Sorrel.
Oxalis Acetosella.
The crimson-veined white wood-sorrel is quite a different character, and is altogether lovely. Each of the five white petals are veined with about half a dozen delicate red lines, which give the flower a decorative appearance; in fact, I have often used it in decorative designs where delicate coloring was employed. Fra Angelico and Sandro Botticelli painted this flower in the foregrounds of their pictures, and it is evident that it looked the same over four hundred years ago as it does to-day. All around the edge of Profile Lake in the Franconia Notch this pretty flower can be found about the end of June and the first of July. It likes the damp woodland best, and can be found on many of the White Moun-

Oxalis Stricta.

Oxalis Acetosella.

72 FAMILIAR FLOWERS OF FIELD AND GARDEN.

tains at an altitude of two thousand feet. Some people mistake the flower for an anemone; but so pronounced a cloverlike leaf is enough to upset any such random conjecture. The flower stem, which grows about three inches high, bears but one blossom.

Sheep Sorrel.
Rumex Acetosella.

Sheep sorrel is a wretch of a weed, which will flourish in sandy or sterile ground, and is the bane of the farmer who tries to raise clover for his cattle. Sorrel seed is so much like clover seed that the two get mixed up sometimes, to the utter discouragement of the farmer. I think the plant ought to be called farmer's-bane. It belongs to the Buckwheat family, and so can claim no relationship with wood sorrel, which belongs to the Geranium family. I have seen a whole field as ruddy-looking as though it were filled with honest, ripe buckwheat, yet the pretty terra-cotta color was produced by the

Sheep Sorrel.

flowering of this miserable sheep sorrel. The weed is so common everywhere that my drawing is sufficient without further description for its identification.

MAY, JUNE, AND JULY. 73

Blue Flag. The larger blue flag grows in the
Iris versicolor. swamp of some rich meadow, or beside the sluggish stream, and shows its lovely variegated, blue-violet flowers in June or early July. The charm of the iris lies in the delicate rich veining of the pale purple-blue petal, or, correctly speaking, larger perianth division; for the iris, or *fleur-de-lis*, is a tube-shaped flower like the morning-glory, and has no petals. Under the microscope its coloring is marvelously beautiful; the bold staining of the waxlike lips, the soft gradation of yellow and white, and the rich purple veining are glorious beyond description. No wonder the handsome, decorative flower attracted the early attention of a Frenchman,

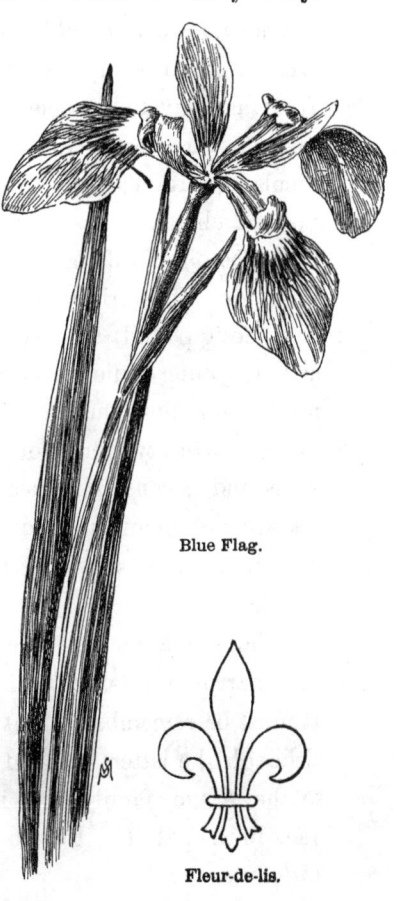

Blue Flag.

Fleur-de-lis.

although how and when still remain historically uncertain; but as early as the time of Charles IV the *fleur-de-lis* began to appear on the banners of France. I have drawn the conventional form of the flower, so our wild specimen may be compared with it. However, the French emblem was copied from a cultivated species whose inner perianth divisions were large and stood in a nearly perpendicular position; our wild specimen lacks this important climax to its beauty, and slightly resembles the *Kœmpferi* (Japanese) *iris*, which is quite flat in figure. The iris is admirably adapted to decorative design, and the wonder is that some of our artistic young ladies who are so skillful with the needle do not employ it oftener in embroidery; the opportunity here for a charming harmony of blues and greens is immeasurable. Blue wild flowers are not plentiful, and the perpetuation in our memories of this one seems to me especially desirable.

There is a slender blue flag (*I. Virginica*), with very narrow leaves, which is also common in swamps. It must be remembered that blue flag is not *Calamus*, although the latter is called sweet flag; this belongs to the Arum family, and is therefore a relation of Jack-in-the-pulpit. Its botanical name is *Acorus Calamus*.

MAY, JUNE, AND JULY.

Arrow-head.
Sagittaria variabilis.
The little water plant called arrow-head blooms in summer beside streamlets and good-sized rivers, where it chooses a locality of a secluded and muddy nature; consequently it is rather inaccessible. It is too beautiful, though, to neglect on account of its surroundings; the extreme delicacy of its three-petaled blossom can scarcely be equaled by any other wild flower. It is well adapted to decorative design, and one of the handsomest effects of coloring may be produced in silk embroidery by representing the beautiful leaf in various shades of green on a water-blue ground, with the graceful, white flower-spikes plentifully woven in between the leaves.

Sabbatia.
Sabbatia chloroides.
One of our most beautiful Eastern wild flowers is *Sabbatia chloroides;* its corolla is magenta-pink, and commonly has eight divisions. It frequents the edges of ponds, and blooms in summer.

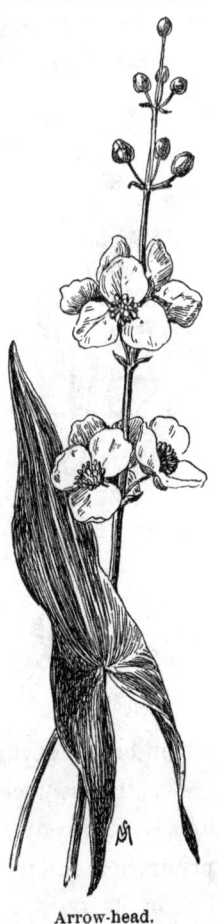

Arrow-head.

Sundrops, or Evening-Primrose.
Œnothera pumila.

The evening-primrose is a four-petaled, pale-yellow flower which one may generally find on the roadside in early summer, or later. The variety *Œ. pumila* I find very common on the meadows of Campton in June. I have drawn a small piece of the plant, to show what is the general appearance of the flowers; they are small and not nearly so pretty as the blossoms of the later-blooming variety we most often meet beside the road.

Evening-Primrose.
Œnothera biennis.

The larger evening-primrose is common beside the road and in the pasture. It has a very lovely, pale, pure yellow blossom without a trace of orange on its petal. The peculiarity of this flower is that it opens about sunset, gives out a faint perfume, and then when broad daylight returns looks limp and withered; this is true also of the charming *Nicotiana affinis* (tobacco). Of course, on cloudy days the primrose looks in better condition; but its only fault lies in its frailty. As a garden flower it is satisfac-

Sundrops.

tory just as portulaca is; but neither the evening-primrose nor the bright-hued portulaca are satisfactory flowers to pick. The tall, straight-stemmed plant has an average height of three feet. It blooms all summer.

Wild Geranium. The wild ge-
Geranium ranium, which
maculatum. the English
usually call wild cranesbill, is a pale purple flower about as delicate in character as the evening-primrose; some botanists do not hesitate to call its color pink. But Gray is right—it is light purple. I found it growing by the roadside, its dainty purple flowers in company with the yellow blossoms of the pretty cinquefoil. The plant grows about fifteen inches high; its leafage is light green, with portions spotty and brownish-looking, and the unopened

Evening-Primrose.

green buds are quite fuzzy. Under a magnifying glass the flowers are very beautiful; the tiny anthers,

Wild Geranium.

instead of being the usual orange-color, are peacock-blue. Seen through the microscope, this blue pollen is quite a curiosity. The plant is in its prime in early June.

Herb Robert.
Geranium Robertianum.

There is another variety of the geranium called herb Robert (*G. Robertianum*). This is also common, and blossoms in June, continuing through the summer. The flowers are nearly magenta color—that is, a deep purple, brownish crimson. The stems of the plant are ruddy.

Indian Poke, or False White Hellebore.
Veratrum viride.

About the end of May or the beginning of June large masses of light green, corrugated leaves are seen in the hollows of the meadow, which have a tropical look. This plant is the Indian poke, and we learn from the farmers that it is poisonous; sheep and pigs have been killed by eating the leaves. Gray says the roots yield the acrid poisonous veratrin. A Campton farmer told me that in his boyhood he innocently fed his father's pigs with some of the plants, and on the following morning they were found "stone dead." The leaves bear a distant resemblance to those of the Funkia (a relative of the poisonous plant); but beyond its leaves it does not interest us; the green flowers are borne on a weedy, pyramidal spike. In later summer the whole plant withers, blackens, and disappears. We are reminded of the ungodly man in David's psalm:

"I went by, and lo, he was gone: I sought him, but his place could nowhere be found."

CHAPTER VI.

MAY, JUNE, JULY, AND AUGUST.
Hobble-bush to Phlox.

Hobble-bush.
Viburnum lantanoides.

THE hobble-bush is a very familiar object of the summer season in the woods of the White Mountains. On the slopes of Mount Osceola, in Waterville, the bush occupies whole acres of ground, and as a forest under-

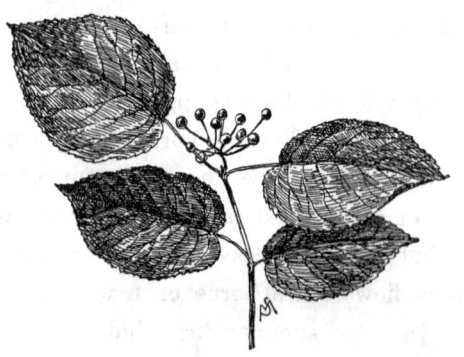

Hobble-bush.

growth scarcely twenty inches high, its round ovate leaves and hydrangealike flowers form an ideally decorative feature of the woods in May. In August the bushes are quite as beautiful when the blossoms are replaced by the coral-red berries; and they are the cheery companions of my long tramps through the hills. But I have never experienced the annoyance of being tripped up by the loops which Gray says are formed by the reclining branches taking root at the end; this is the reason why it is called hobble-bush.

Bunch-berry. The bunch-berry is one of the most
Cornus Canadensis. conspicuous and beautiful objects which meets one's eyes, when, after a weary climb, the mountain top is at last gained. The bunches of bright scarlet berries encircled by a cluster of about six light green, ovate pointed leaves are irresistibly attractive, and one must leave the path to gather some. In early June the pretty little flower is quite interesting for several reasons; what seem to be four white petals, two of which are smaller than the others, are not petals at all, but involucre leaves. The flowers are tiny little greenish things with black dots in between. An examination of the flowers under the microscope

Bunch-berry.

will at once make the tiny forms clear. The scarlet berries are quite insipid to the taste.

Partridge-berry. In a certain spot on the slope of a
Mitchella repens. hill, and covering a bowlder imbedded in the swamp which is encircled by a group of hemlocks, I always find a splendid mass of partridge-berry vines, too lovely for rude hands to disturb, somewhere about the 1st of May. Then the pretty double berries of a brilliant shiny scarlet are plentifully dotted over the dark-green leaves just forsaken by the winter's snow! It is not until June that the little twin blossoms appear; these are sweet-scented and pink-tipped, and remind one somewhat of attenuated arbutus blossoms.

Partridge-berry.

Blossoms of Partridge-berry.

Goldthread. Goldthread is popular among
Coptis trifolia. the New England farmers' wives, who use the slender yellow roots for medicinal purposes. But this fact is scarcely as interesting as the bright and shiny dark-green leaf which holds its color all winter, and in summer carpets the wet woods. The flowers are small and anemonelike, and appear in early spring; but the leaves are sym-

metrical and beautiful, somewhat wedge-shaped, and in three divisions. The wiry, yellow roots make identification perfectly easy.

Shepherd's-Purse.
Capsella Bursa-Pastoris.
The shepherd's-purse is, as Gray says, the commonest kind of a weed, yet I must say that in all my extended rambles through the White Hills it was not found! Never having instigated a search for the insignificant weed, possibly it would take but a little while to secure a specimen; but what I say remains true in reference to certain localities in the New Hampshire hills—the weed is not common there! I remember as a boy that at Hastings-on-the-Hudson it grew everywhere, and we used to call it peppergrass because it had a stingy taste. The small white flowers hardly deserve attention, but the seed pod is interesting on account of the triangular, pouch-shape which gave rise to the common name. This weed blooms all summer. Our beautiful garden candytuft is its rich relation—that is, the riches lie in the flowers, and not in the "purse"; but the similarity of the seed pods of these two plants is apparent at a glance.

Wild Mustard.
Brassica (or Sinapis) nigra.
The wild mustard, generally called black mustard, with small, pale, pure yellow flowers, is a familiar object in nearly all the fields of Campton. It is quite common, and its straggling, spreading stems are in bloom all

84 FAMILIAR FLOWERS OF FIELD AND GARDEN.

summer, but is scarcely interesting enough to deserve attention while so many other more beautiful flowers are in our midst.

Stagger-bush.
Andromeda Mariana.
The stagger-bush grows in low ground eastward and south, but I have never found it in New Hampshire. The tiny flowers, less than half an inch long, are cylindrical in shape, and are sometimes tinged faintly with pink. So dainty a flower must surely attract those to whom it is not a familiar object; the blossom slightly resembles the wintergreen or checkerberry flower, to which it is closely related, and the glossy olive-green leaf is said to be poisonous to lambs and calves. The flowers will be found in late spring and early summer, on the slender woody stems of a bush about three feet high. The shrub has

Stagger-bush.

MAY, JUNE, JULY, AND AUGUST. 85

lately been cultivated for purposes of garden adornment.

Mountain Laurel. The mountain laurel is not strictly
Kalmia latifolia. confined to mountain districts; on
the contrary, if my experience is like that of others,
the most beautiful specimens are oftenest gathered
from flat land like that of Long Island and the "Pines" of New Jersey. There does not seem to be any in the Pemigewasset Valley in the White Mountains; and the supply on the shores of Squam Lake in the southern district of the hills is very limited. Certainly

Mountain Laurel.

Kalmia latifolia is the most conventionally beautiful wild flower we possess, yet it is rarely if ever a success transplanted to cultivated grounds. Unless its natural environment is exactly repeated in its new quarters, it invariably pines away and dies.

It certainly will not endure the savage violence of a New England coast climate; it prefers the equable temperature of the pine district of New Jersey. In some parts of the latter State the bushes grow to a height of ten feet or more, and in the mountains of Pennsylvania they grow fully twenty feet high. The perfect, waxlike flower is arranged on the plan of a wheel, with the stamens representing the spokes; these are arched, and are so elastic that when the tips are released from the little notch in the corolla (the anther is held there temporarily) the pollen is fired right or left, as a boy would sling a green apple from the sharpened end of a supple stick; this is an ingenious bit of Nature's artifice by which she secures cross-fertilization. Of course, a visiting insect experiences a perfect bombardment of yellow pollen when it alights on a flower, occasioned by its walking on the stamens and knocking them out of place; then, powdered over like a dusty miller, it visits another flower, and Nature's little scheme is carried out to perfection! It is worth while to spend a few minutes in a garden watching a clumsy bumblebee; the process of pollen transfer will then be easily understood. As a boy, I found it amusing to liberate the stamens of a *Kalmia* blossom with the point of a pin, and watch the

MAY, JUNE, JULY, AND AUGUST. 87

yellow pollen fly. Nothing is more beautiful then the golden forms of the dainty pollen specks under the microscope. The flowers are in their prime in June, when they will tinge a whole hillside with pinkish white. The full flower is usually pure white, and the undeveloped, ornamental bud a very pronounced pink. *Kalmia glauca* (common in the North) is a variety with small lilac-colored flowers.

Sheep Laurel.

Sheep Laurel.
Kalmia angustifolia.
The sheep laurel is not nearly as large as the mountain laurel, nor is it as beautiful; but the blossoms are decidedly pink, and are daintily formed. I find it in bloom

as late as the end of June in Campton; but it is so very uncommon there that it can only be found in two places, so far as my knowledge extends. New Hampshire certainly is not rich in *Kalmia*, for when one has to hunt for a flower it can not be called common. As Gray calls its color crimson-purple, I must draw attention to the fact that there is never any *purple* in it, but that the true color is a delicate crimson-pink. It grows in the poor soil of rather low grounds.

Candytuft. The cheery garden candytuft is a member of the Mustard family, and a near relative of the common weed, shepherd's-purse. It is a captivating little flower which is in constant bloom from June until October, winning every heart by its untiring courage in meeting all conditions of weather with fresh relays of its dainty white or purple flowers. It is astonishing to note in advanced autumn that the little plants have not yet spent all their energy; all they ask is that their flowers should be picked, and a new supply takes the place of the old. I find that the

Iberis umbellata.

Dobbie's Double Spiral Candytuft.

most satisfactory variety is Dobbie's Double Spiral; the Rocket is also good, but it does not produce such large flower-heads as the former variety. Candytuft comes to us from Europe, and gets its botanical name from Iberia, the old name for Spain. I have found a very beautiful variety of the flower growing wild on the rocky slopes of Gibraltar. There is a white perennial variety called *I. sempervirens;* *I. Gibraltica* is the same under cultivation; its flowers are white, crimson, and rose-color. Some of us may be surprised to learn that Gibraltar has an extensive flora; it is far from being a barren rock. In the short climb up the path from the town to the fortifications I picked as many as fifteen specimens of unfamiliar wild flowers besides a dozen or so which I recognized as old friends; this was on the first day of March, too! Dr. Henry M. Field says: "Gibraltar is not a barren cliff; its very crags are mantled with vegetation, and wild flowers spring up almost as in Palestine. Those who have made a study of its flora tell us that it has no less than five hundred species of flowering plants and ferns, of which but one tenth have been brought from abroad; all the rest are native."

Sweet Alyssum. Sweet alyssum is like mignonette
Alyssum maritimum. in one respect—its qualities surpass its charms. It has small, white, honey-scented flow-

ers with an odor like that of buckwheat; it comes to us from Europe ; a variety common in garden borders has small, ornamental, pale-green leaves white-edged. Alyssum is also a member of the Mustard family, and is closely allied to candytuft and shepherd's-purse. It blooms all summer.

Cornflower, or Bachelor's Button.
Centaurea Cyanus.
The bluest of all blue flowers, the cornflower or bachelor's button, vies with the gentian which Bryant seems to consider a most perfect blue; but a flower of the *true* blue does not exist; it is only suggested by the forget-me-not. There is too much purple in the cornflower for us to indulge in praises of its blue. For all that, its color is still charming, and in Germany (the flower originally came to us from that country), where it grows wild in the wheat fields, the harmony of its blue with the straw-yellow is æsthetically perfect. But the cornflower shows us other colors than blue; there are light and deep crimson-pink, purple and violet, both these colors striped with white, lilac, and white with pink or with blue center. Its foliage is a soft, silvery, whitish green, and its bloom is continuous and prolific through the early summer; it blooms quite as well if planted later in the season, and is an annual highly prized in old-fashioned gardens. A comparison of the *Centaureas* with ironweed and blazing-star, which are distant relatives, is interesting,

as there are some curious points of resemblance in the general appearance of the flowers. *C. odorata* (sweet sultan) is closely allied to the cornflower, and it bears yellow as well as pink and purple flowers. *C. moschata*, a musk-scented variety, has magenta-pink and white flowers. *C. sauveolens* is a beautiful, pure yellow flower which assumes showy proportions under greenhouse care. All these are annuals and natives of Asia. The dusty miller, which is so common as a white-leaved plant for garden borders, is a perennial variety which is again separated into varieties named *C. candidissima*, *C. clementei*, and *C. gymnocarpa*. These possess no important distinguishing differences which are of interest here.

Mignonette. Our common garden mignonette *Reseda odorata.* comes from the Levant, and is an annual cultivated for the sweet scent of its tiny, rusty and greenish-white flowers—it is the anthers which are rust-color; the rest of the rather uninteresting flower assumes a variety of greenish tints, which are quite beautiful under the microscope. There is one relative of the mignonette in this country which grows wild along the roadsides, but it is not very common; it is named *R. luteola*. It is a tall weed with lance-shaped leaves and a long spike of small, dull-yellowish flowers which slightly remind one of the white golden-rod. In Italy, among the mountains, and in Gibraltar there are two wild species of mignonette, each tiny in figure but having the unmistakable family look; they are *R. sesamonides* and *R. glauca*. Mignonette is an annual with the happy faculty of blooming all summer long; it wastes its sweetness, not "on the desert air," but in the farmhouse kitchen and the fashionable drawing-room. It is a simple flower with the charm of perfect sweetness, a quality quite lacking in many a showy flower, and the sandier the soil is, the sweeter it grows.

Phlox Drummondii,
Annual.
Phlox decussata,
Perennial.

Phlox is the Greek name for fire, and, although all the phloxes are not fiery-hued, there are many of them brilliant and red enough to deserve the name. They are North American plants, and the annual variety comes from Texas. The range of color in the Drummond phlox is extraordinary. There are cream-white, pale yellow, pale salmon-pink, deep pink, crimson-pink, magenta, purple, lilac, pure red, crimson, and solferino. But there is no orange nor scarlet. The five divisions of the corolla are often starry-eyed, and sometimes they are striped; in the varieties *cuspidata* and *fimbriata* they are slashed and toothed in a remarkable way. The star-shaped flowers are curiously marked with color, and the corolla is often so deeply incised that the flower is no longer recognizable as the sober flatdisked phlox of bygone days. In truth, I might add that star phlox (called Star of Quedlinburg) is one of the curiosities of the modern garden. The seed is slow to germinate, and the little plants take a long time to grow, but eventually they reward us with a plentiful and continuous bloom which is more than a liberal payment for the small amount of care bestowed upon them. They begin to flower in June, and about the last of October Jack Frost claims the last lingering blossoms. *P. decussata*, the perennial variety under cultivation, is not quite so brilliant in coloring, but it is refined and delicate, and has the advantage of permanency. Its strongest and best hues are crimson, magenta, and pink. *P. maculata* is a wild variety of the South and West, with a pyramidal cluster of pale magenta or white

White Phlox Drummondii.

flowers, and purple-brown spotted, lance-shaped lower leaves; it flowers in summer. *P. divaricata* is a graceful variety which is found in the same part of the country, but in moist localities, and has loose spreading clusters of large lilac and bluish lilac flowers which appear in late spring; it has been crossed in cultivation, and is found in the garden in larger figure and finer colors. *P. glaberrima* and *P. Carolina* are pink and pale-pink varieties which are common in the near West and South, and flower in early summer. The five lobes of the corolla are round. The former variety has slender stems, long lance-shaped leaves, and loose flower clusters; the latter, stout stems, ovate or even heart-shaped leaves, and crowded flower clusters. *P. subulata* is a low-creeping little plant, so entirely different from the foregoing varieties that I have given it separate consideration elsewhere. These wild phloxes are all perennials, and they have been more or less introduced into the garden, where they appear in so many varied types that they are not easily recognized. The most satisfactory color in the perennial flowers is white; the pale magenta tints of some others are not very beautiful.

Star of Quedlinburg.

CHAPTER VII.

MAY, JUNE, JULY, AND AUGUST.

Caraway to Indian Cucumber Root.

Caraway.
Carum Carui.

THE caraway has found its way into the fields and pastures from the kitchen garden, and has really become a very familiar wild flower in many parts of the country. It might possibly be mistaken for wild carrot on account of the similar gray-white flowers, but the resemblance is too superficial to deserve attention. My drawing shows the superior delicacy of the caraway flowers; indeed, they are as beautiful as some varieties of *Spiræa*. The plant grows about twenty inches high, and blooms

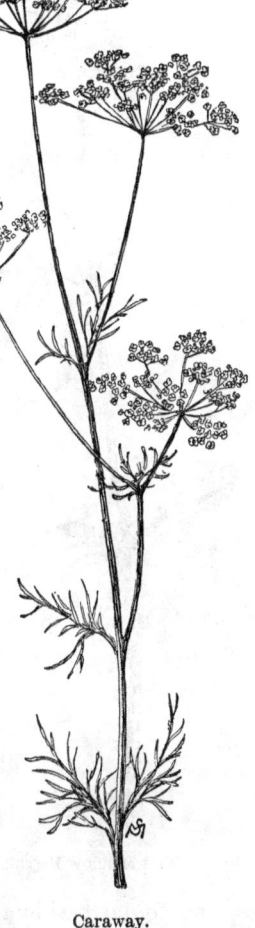

Caraway.

about the middle of June. Its aromatic seeds are used plentifully to flavor the familiar New York New-Year's cake.

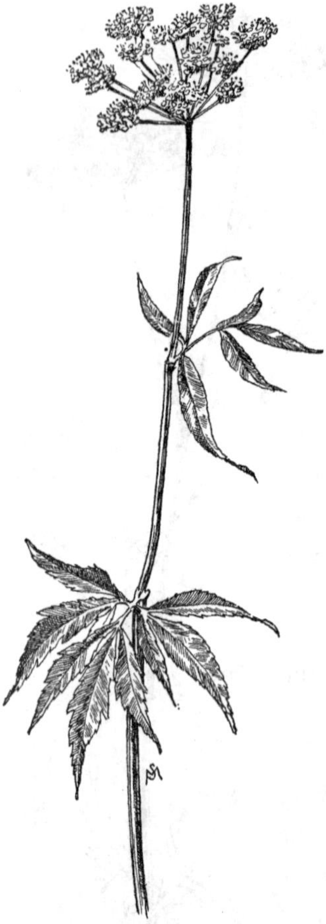

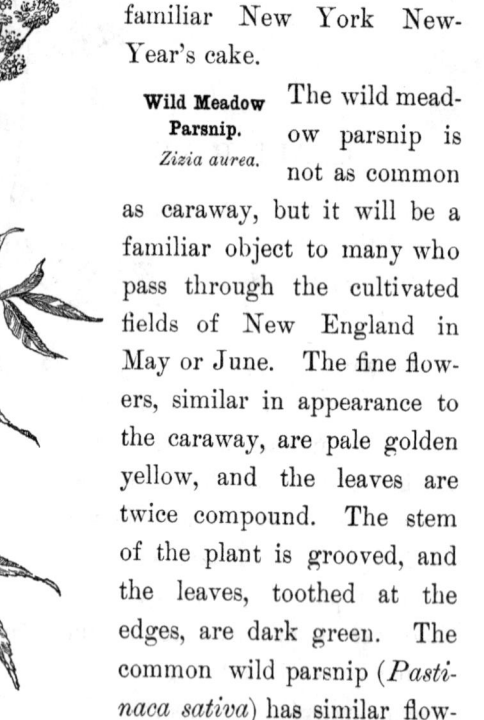

Wild Meadow Parsnip.
Zizia aurea.

The wild meadow parsnip is not as common as caraway, but it will be a familiar object to many who pass through the cultivated fields of New England in May or June. The fine flowers, similar in appearance to the caraway, are pale golden yellow, and the leaves are twice compound. The stem of the plant is grooved, and the leaves, toothed at the edges, are dark green. The common wild parsnip (*Pastinaca sativa*) has similar flowers, but the stem is heavier and deeper grooved, and its leaves are simply compound.

Bush-Honeysuckle.
Diervilla trifida.

The bush-honeysuckle will be found beside the road and in the hedges, where

Wild Meadow Parsnip.

MAY, JUNE, JULY, AND AUGUST. 97

it may be recognized at once by its small honey-yellow flowers rather than by its leaves, which are not different from a great many others with whose company they are pretty sure to be well mixed. There is only a slight resemblance to the cultivated honeysuckle in this wild variety; and beside the magnificent pink blossoms of the *D. Japonica*, that beautiful shrub which comes to us from Japan, our native variety dwindles into utter insignificance. It blooms in early summer.

Mountain Sandwort.
Arenaria Grœnlandica.

On the top of Mount Washington, seeking shelter in the crevices of the storm-beaten rocks, one may find in early summer plenty of the dainty little Alpine plant called mountain sandwort; it is sometimes called mountain

Bush-Honeysuckle.

98 FAMILIAR FLOWERS OF FIELD AND GARDEN.

daisy by the people of that locality. The flower grows about three inches high on a fine stem, and is tiny and dainty; each petal is notched at the end, and is translucent white in color. Little specimens of the plant are tucked into small birch-bark baskets and sold to the visitors on the mountain. Of course, it gets its name by its arctic preferences; for the cold fog, snow, and ice of Greenland are its natural environment. Still, we are surprised at finding such a delicate-looking little thing on the bleak, desolate summit of the great New England mountain.

Mountain Sandwort.

Indian Pipe. Gray's description of the Indian
Monotropa uniflora. pipe is so simple that I can not do better than quote what he says: "Common Indian pipe, or corpse plant; in rich woods, smooth, waxy-white all over, three to six inches high, with one rather large nodding flower of five petals and ten stamens." These are what might be called the bare facts of its existence. But there is more that is really interesting about it: the queer, little, un-

canny thing flourishes on decay; it grows parasitically on the roots of other plants, and we may find it oftenest beside the decayed stump of some forest giant, where its pearly whiteness is relieved against a background of decaying, moss-covered wood. The flower sometimes has a faint pink flush on its face, but is oftenest as pale as death. There is something weirdly suggestive in its deathliness: why should it have been named Indian pipe? It occurred to me once, when I was climbing the slopes of South Mountain in the Catskills and came across a pretty group of the ghostly little pipes, that they were wrongly named; they should have been called the Pipes of Hudson's Crew. Those of us who have seen the ghostly crew in Jefferson's Rip Van Winkle can easily imagine the gnomelike creatures smoking pale pipes like these. But the weird little plant is as curious in death as it is in life, for immediately

Indian Pipe.

after being picked it begins to blacken, and (most curious contradiction) a pressed specimen of the pearly white flower eventually becomes "as black as your hat." Indian pipe grows in the deep woods in early summer. *Monotropa Hypopitys*, or false beech-drops, closely related to the pale Indian pipe, has a ruddy complexioned, fragrant, and small (generally four-petaled) flower which blooms in the pine woods in summer.

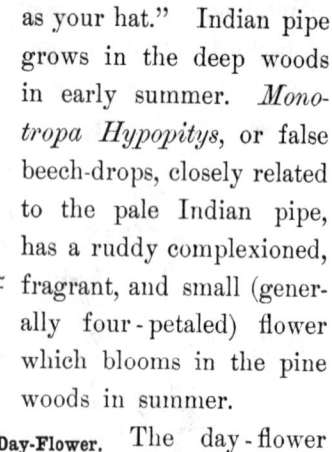

Common Day-Flower. The day-flower
Commelina Virginica. is common in our Eastern seaboard States from New York to Florida, and blooms in summer. It has light violet-blue flowers, irregular in shape, and three-petaled; three stamens project considerably beyond the petals. The flowers seem to grow out from an upper spathelike leaf, and the leaves are lance-shaped and contracted at the base. The plant is a near relative of the spiderwort, and like the latter has a peculiar mucilaginous juice.

Common Day-Flower.

Spiderwort.
Tradescantia Virginica.

The spiderwort, somewhat more familiar to us in the old-fashioned garden than growing wild, is nevertheless common in some of the moist places of western New York and the South. It is an attractive little, three-petaled, purple-blue flower with orange-yellow anthers, which unfortunately has a very short life. There are so few blue wild flowers that the delicate blossom is beautiful for this reason if for no other. The little blue clusters snuggled at the bases of the narrow green leaves form a very pretty bit of color harmony. The plant blooms in early summer.

Star of Bethlehem.
Ornithogalum umbellatum.

Spiderwort.

Gray says the star of Bethlehem is an old garden flower which has escaped to low meadows. The leaves are long and grasslike, and the flower, like that of *Nicotiana affinis*, is white within and green without; but, exactly *unlike* the latter flower, it opens in sunshine. It is common in some localities and absent in others; it grows, for instance, in the fields around Morristown, N. J., and also in Prospect Park, Brooklyn; but I have never found it in the meadows of New Hampshire. It is a near relative of the dog's-tooth violet, but blooms much later, in early summer. It belongs to the Lily family.

Buttercup. The child's favorite yellow wild flow-
Ranunculus repens. er, the buttercup, does not need any hints or facts recorded here for its identification; yet I wish to draw a closer attention to the flower. Those artistically inclined young people who like to paint the familiar buttercup frequently lose sight of its simple elements of beauty; I allude to the shape of the leaf and the burnished color of the flower. The leaf is one of the most charming instances of symmetry in Nature. Examine it closely, and, for the sake of better acquaintance, spread a large perfect specimen flatly on a piece of paper, trace around its edge with a sharp-pointed pencil, and note the conventional, decorative beauty of the outline thus obtained. There are not many flowers which can boast of such a beautiful leaf. Then the brilliant yellow of the corolla is almost beyond the power of pure water color to reproduce. The only way one can adequately represent it is to use the purest yellow, and leave, for the dazzling touches of light, spots of the clean white paper beneath. The

finest buttercups frequent moist meadow land, and they are in their prime in June and July. *R. fascicularis* is an early variety of the buttercup, which grows in rocky pastures and is about six inches high.

Dandelion.
Taraxacum Dens-leonis.
The common dandelion, which stars the meadows in May and June with its radiant circles of gold, would be a garden favorite were it less common. But this prodigality of gold unfortunately fails to arouse the interest of older people; only children appreciate this kind of riches. They must study the heart of the flower who would see the gold in its depths. A big dandelion placed under the magnifying glass is one of the grandest studies in golden yellow that can be imagined. The richness of color which is occasioned by the crowding together of such a number of brilliant yellow florets (for it must be remembered that the dandelion is a group of individual flowers) is beyond description. Yet we pass the common flower with perfect indifference; but there was one man who did not. It was Lowell, who said:

" Dear common flower, that grow'st beside the way,
    Fringing the dusty road with harmless gold,
  First pledge of blithesome May,
    Which children pluck, and, full of pride, uphold,

> High-hearted buccaneers, o'erjoyed that they
>   An El Dorado in the grass have found,
>   Which not the rich earth's ample round
> May match in wealth—thou art more dear to me
> Than all the prouder summer blooms may be."

This is the first verse of the only poem which perfectly celebrates the magnificent golden color of the dandelion. It is indeed childhood's favorite flower, and the beautiful lines express the feeling in the heart of every true flower lover, old or young. What the world might call *common* was something infinitely more to Lowell. Only a poet could so perfectly estimate the wisdom of a child who looks " on the living pages of God's book," while grown-up people pass them by.

The largest and handsomest dandelions I have ever seen grow in Nantucket; the farther north one goes the smaller the flower grows. There is another dandelion, a fall flower (*Leontodon autumnale*), which will be noticed further on. I must not omit to mention the Cynthia dandelion (*Krigia dandelion*), which is common from March to July in moist ground from Maryland west to Kansas, and from there southwardly to Texas. Prof. Meehan says: " The flowers are open before the frosts are wholly gone; and before March has departed the yellow buds break forth in all their spring beauty and clothe the meadows with their brilliant flowers." It is well to know that the common dandelion is not a native of our country, but was brought here by the white man, with whom it soon made a home on the red man's lands.

Ox-eye Daisy.
Chrysanthemum Leucanthemum.

The familiar daisy which is so much beloved of the children is really a chrysanthemum, very closely related to the magnificent golden flower of Japan, which has reached such gigantic proportions through cultivation. In early summer the fields are white with the flower, and its presence in the grass is so annoying to the farmer that it has been called farmer's curse. Still, for all that, the golden-eyed, white-rayed little thing is æsthetically perfect, and artists as well as children love the flower for its own sweet simplicity. The little pink English daisy is only cousin to our daisy; in fact, it is not a chrysanthemum, and it does not grow wild in our country as it does in England and on the Continent. The ox-eye daisy, like the dandelion, was brought to this country by the white man. It blooms in early summer. A near relative of the daisy, which flowers in June, is the pyrethrum (*C. Parthenium*), which has run wild, especially in New York, from old gardens. It has loose clusters of crimson-pink or white flowers, in form resembling the ox-eye daisy. The variety under cultivation called *Roseum* supplies us with the well-known Persian insect powder. *C. parthenioides*, or double-flowered feverfew, is another relative of the ox-eye daisy. Its pure white, rounded flowers, about the size of a nickel, are commonly seen in our gardens in summer and early autumn. They resemble the English daisy (*Bellis*) in form, but have no pink tinge.

Heliotrope.
Heliotropium Peruvianum.

The beautiful, sweet-scented heliotrope comes from Peru and Chili. It is a perennial held in high esteem by all; hardly a farmhouse window which holds a few flowering geraniums is without its treasured pot of heliotrope; and the conservatories might all boast of many fine specimens. The name comes from the Greek, and means turning to the sun. There are several variations of its color, from light to dark purple, and even white; but the darker colors are most beautiful. M. Lemoine, of France, has raised some of the finest varieties. An essence of heliotrope is used as perfumery; but among our flowers the most fragrant ones, strange as it may seem, are the least available for

Heliotrope.

their perfume; in such a case a "fixing scent," such as neroli, vanilla, orris, or musk, is generally employed, and this is supposed to strike the same "key" on the olfactory nerve as the real essence, and also to change its volatility to permanence; thus vanilla is used as a basis for heliotrope perfume. There are great flower farms in the south of France devoted to the interests of French perfumery. Violets are imitated by attar of almonds, tuberose, and orris; orris is obtained from the Florentine iris (*I. Florentina*). Heliotrope blooms from early summer onward.

Atamasco Lily. The Atamasco *Amaryllis Atamasco.* lily, sometimes called zephyr flower, or zephyranthes, is a native of the South, common in low grounds, and is now cultivated in the garden, where it blooms in early summer; its flowers are pure pink, or white. In my garden I notice they seem to bloom hurriedly or not at all.

Atamasco Lily.

The flower appears (quite as soon as the broad, grasslike leaves) in the Carolinas and southward from March to June, according to the locality. It is a relative of the yellow star-grass and the snowdrop. To this family also belong the common English daffodil (*N. Pseudo-Narcissus*), the jonquil (*N. jonquilla*), and the *Narcissi poeticus* and *polyanthos;* this last, a variety of tiny flowers in clusters, I have found growing wild in Switzerland near the St. Bernard Pass, in May; it is the parent of the cultivated variety named *N. Tazetta*, or *Polyanthus Narcissus*. But these are more successful as hot-house plants, although some are quite hardy in gardens south of Boston.

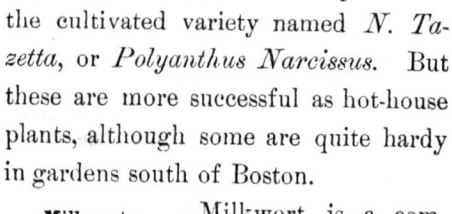

Milkwort.
Polygala sanguinea.

Milkwort is a common weed which generally grows in wet sandy ground and bears pinkish-crimson flowers in a head somewhat similar to clover, but smaller. It grows not more than nine inches high, and is common in Massachusetts and in the pine district of New Jersey, in the vicinity of Lakewood. Its name was derived from two Greek words, meaning much milk; not that the plants yielded milky juice, but it was thought that

Polygala Sanguinea.

in pasturage they increased the milk of cows. The milkwort flowers all summer.

Seneca Snakeroot. Senega, or seneca snakeroot, is anoth-
Polygala Senega. er member of the Polygala family, which is common in the West. Its flowers are white and small, and are clustered in a simple terminal spike. The plant is about ten inches high, and the lance-ovate leaves follow the stem in alternate positions; the flowers appear in late spring. Senega is used for medicinal purposes, and is often given in the form of a sirup for a cough. *P. polygama* is still another common variety of milkwort, which is found in sandy places. Its insignificant crimson-pink flowers, of a deep hue, are hardly as handsome as Gray would lead us to suppose. But the useful, fertile flowers of this plant are borne on short underground runners, and are still less conspicuous. The little plant blooms all summer. *P. lutea* is an orange-yellow variety common in sandy swamps southward. Its leaves grow alternately on a low stem which is terminated by a single flower head.

Indian The Indian cucumber-root, which re-
Cucumber-Root. ceives its name from the taste of the
Medeola Virginica. tuberous, horizontal, and white root stalk, flowers in early summer; but the blossom is very unattractive, and it is only in September, when the beautiful dark purple berries appear in clusters of

three, that our attention is attracted to the plant. It grows in the woods, and has a simple stem with a circle of six or seven thin, parallel-ribbed, bright green leaves; close up to the berries are three smaller leaves.

Indian Cucumber-Root.

CHAPTER VIII.

JUNE, JULY, AND AUGUST.

Nasturtium to Purple-flowering Raspberry.

Nasturtium, or Indian Cress.
Tropæolum.

The nasturtium is perhaps one of the most satisfactory of all the garden annuals; it produces an immense number of flowers with a small amount of attention from the gardener, and it withstands drought and the intense heat of midsummer better than any other denizen of the garden. The flower comes to us from South America, chiefly from Peru and Chili. No wonder that it is well adapted to a climate subject to hot waves and drought. Although the fruit is pickled, and finds its way to our tables as an agreeable condiment, the flowers oftener appear there as a midsummer decoration. What a glory of color it brings us!—golden yellow, palest straw-color, the

N. Prince Henry.

same tint with ruby eyes, rich maroon, burning scarlet, intense red, scarlet pink, delicate salmon, russet-orange, bright orange, æsthetic old gold, and gray-purple in silky sheen, peach-blow pink, streaky bronze and gold, ruby-eyed gold, and a host of variations of all these colors which I never could adequately describe in twenty pages. The varieties which seem to me most attractive are, in order, as follows:

Prince Henry,	Streaked scarlet and straw-yellow.
Empress of India,	Intense red, dark foliage.
Aurora,	Salmon and orange-buff.
Pearl,	Pale straw-yellow.
Rose,	Deep scarlet-lake pink.
Edward Otto,	Pale brownish lilac.
King of Tom Thumbs,	Intense scarlet, dark foliage.
Asa Gray,	Straw-yellow, striped with dull red.

For a really beautiful dark flower the King Theodore, clothed in velvety maroon, must command our admiration, but the darker and richer Black Scabiosa (mourning bride) is handsomer than the deepest-hued nasturtium. The Crystal Palace Gem, straw-yellow with maroon eyes, is dainty in coloring, but not so delicate in effect as the pale Pearl. What is remarkable about these nasturtiums (all except Edward Otto and Asa Gray belong to the dwarf division, which does not climb) is their prodigality of bloom. From six dozen plants one may gather during the height of bloom fully three hundred flowers each day for a period of two weeks; the picking of about four thousand flowers during so short a time, it is needless to say, would keep one pretty well occupied.

But such results are not to be obtained under any other than favorable conditions: the nasturtium wants all the sun it can get, plenty of water, and nothing but sandy loam to grow in; any richer ground, or lesser sunlight, will make the plant produce nothing but leaves. It is curious to note how quickly the little plant responds to the right kind of treatment: if we wish many flowers, we must not fail to pick each blossom as soon as it appears; if the flowers are allowed to remain on the plant, the latter concludes that they are not wanted, and soon ceases to produce any more; as fast as the flowers are gathered, others begin to make their appearance; whereas, if the plants are left to themselves, there

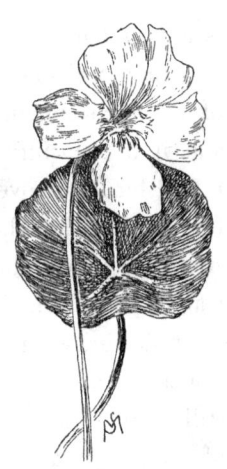

N. Pearl.

N. King Theodore.

is a grand display of color for a very short season and then no flowers at all. The nasturtium is one of the earliest annuals to reward us with its flowers, and it is amusing to see how soon the little humming bird discovers the whereabouts of the first blossom, and how he lingers over it, taking repeated sips of honey, reluctant at last to leave. I have watched one little fellow visit flower after flower, when later in the season they were very plentiful, and, still loath to leave such a paradise of sweets, rest awhile on the wire screen which supported the sweet peas, preening his feathers contentedly, and then make a final round as though he was bent on obtaining a square meal before leaving a certainty for an uncertainty.

N. Asa Gray.

There are three divisions of the nasturtium group which are different in habit of growth : the *dwarf*, which does not climb; the *Lobbianum*, which runs over the ground and climbs very little ; and the *major*, which attains a height of ten feet or more. The dwarf is the most prolific bloomer, but the Lobbianum has a larger and more perfect flower; the major is a splendid variety for climbing over fences, and so forth, and its foliage is of ranker growth. Of these three varieties the dwarf seems most satisfactory, as it requires the least attention, takes the least amount of space, and insures the largest returns; with a hundred plants, carefully set out, one should be able to gather a thousand blossoms a day at the height of the season; this would not be possible with either of the other varieties.

Leaf Canary-Bird Vine.

Tropæolum peregrinum is a very near relative of the nasturtium, and is a beautiful-leafed vine, with rather small, pure yellow flowers; from a fancied resemblance of the blossom to the canary, it is sometimes called canary-bird flower. The vine climbs by means of the leaf stem, which develops a sort of kink in the effort to catch on something and draw itself upward. The leaf is deeply lobed, white-veined, and of a soft, light-green color. The flower has five petals, with the three lower ones fringed. The vine is in bloom all summer. The water-cress (*Nasturtium officinale*), whose botanical name is somewhat misleading, is a member of the Mustard family, and is therefore unrelated to our garden nasturtium.

Balsam, or Lady's Slipper.
Impatiens balsamina.

A close relation of the jewel weed, the garden balsam, or lady's slipper, bears a striking resemblance to the wild species; but only the single flowers look like the jewel weed; the double ones rather resemble the *Camellia Japonica*. Nowadays the horticulturists give us a splendid double flower which has little likeness to the single lady's slippers of our grandmothers' gardens. The variety named Malmaison is a favorite of mine; it has the most delicate blush-pink color imaginable, and certainly looks like the rose it was named for. The balsam comes to us from India. It blooms throughout the summer.

Malmaison Balsam.

Geranium.
Pelargonium.

The name *Pelargonium* is from the Greek word meaning *stork*, and was suggested by the shape of the seed pod, which resembles that of the bird's beak. The wild geranium carries the English name crane's-bill for the same reason. Our *Pelargoniums* are natives of the Cape of Good Hope, and they are so mixed up through crossing in the process of cultivation that only a few species may be identified with the help of botanical descriptions. The following are common in our gardens:

Peppermint P. (*P. tomentosum*).—The leaves are large, round, heart-shaped, with five to seven lobes, and are velvety-hairy on both sides. The insignificant flowers are white. By gentle pressure the leaf will emit a peppermint odor, by which the plant can be easily identified.

Rose-scented P. (*P. capitatum*).—The leaves are velvety, rounded and moderately lobed, and the little flowers, scarcely half an inch long, are of a magenta-crimson color; there are many flowers in a head; the foliage is unmistakably rose-scented.

Pennyroyal P. (*P. exstipulatum*).—This variety has an altogether different leaf from the foregoing; botanically speaking, it is palmately three-parted—i. e., in figure like the triple leaf of the clover, but, unlike the latter, these divisions are close together and wedge-shaped with toothed edges; it is also small, perhaps half an inch wide, and is soft and velvety; it has a strong aromatic smell like pennyroyal. The flowers are very small and white.

All three of these varieties are commonly cultivated by the farmers' wives throughout New York and New England.

Ivy-leaved P. (*P. peltatum*).—This variety has an ivy-shaped, smooth, five-lobed leaf, sometimes with a dark zone, and is easily recognized. The flowers are generally of crimson or cherry tones of color, with a variety of pink tints and also a pure white. I know of only one or two scarlet varieties, and these are of recent introduction.

Horseshoe P. (*P. zonale*) and Stained or Scarlet P. (*P. inquinans*) are two varieties which have become inextricably mixed; the former has a dark horseshoe mark or zone on the leaf, which, however, is sometimes wanting, and the latter has a lighter green leaf without the zone. Both varieties have round scalloped leaves, which have a "fishy smell." To these two classes belong the infinite variety of bright-colored and delicately tinted flowering geraniums which are so common as bedding plants. A notable white variety with double flowers is called La Favorite; a lovely salmon-pink one is the Beauté Poitevine. Nearly all these geraniums have received the close attention of French horticulturists, and in the continuous process of cross-fertilization we have quite lost sight

Leaf of P. Zonal.

of some of the original species. The common sweet-scented geraniums, with small inconspicuous crimson-pink flowers, generally belong to the variety called *P. Radula*.

As a rule, all the mixed, showy-flowered *Pelargoniums* are called Lady Washington geraniums; this name does not apply to any individual variety. One of the most beautiful of the light-leaved geraniums is called Madame Salleroi; the leaf is almost white, and is generally zoned with a pale green.

La Favorite Geranium.

It is interesting to know that the wild geranium, herb Robert, wood sorrel, garden geranium, nasturtium, canary-bird vine, jewel weed, and lady's slipper (balsam) all belong to the Geranium family. It is seldom the case that a family circle includes so many attractive and beautiful individuals who are distinguished by such a marked contrast in character; how widely different the wood sorrel is from the scarlet geranium!

Portulaca.
Portulaca grandiflora.

Portulaca comes to us from South America. Its brilliant flowers, in shape closely resembling a wild rose, are found snuggled close to the ground in nearly every country garden. The foliage is narrow like fir-needles, but of a thick and pulpy nature; the stems are also thick and are ruddy in color. There is a great variety of colors among the flowers—crimson, pure pink, scarlet-pink, magenta, scarlet, pale and deep yellow, buff, and orange. The double variety, in my estimation, is not as beautiful as the single. A troublesome weed of the garden resembling portulaca, but having a broader and blunt leaf, is called *P. oleracea*, purslane, or pusley. Charles Dudley Warner, in My Summer in a Garden, has drawn particular attention to this omnipresent weed; it is a great nuisance to the amateur gardener, but he can console himself with the thought that it was handed down to him from his ancestors; they brought it with them from the old country, and it once supplied the table with a much-relished dish of greens which has since been displaced by spinach and young beet-tops. Portulaca is an annual which flowers all summer.

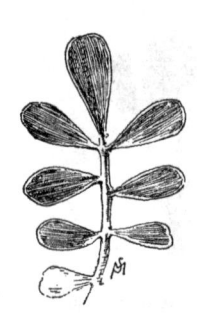

Leaf of Pusley.

Amarantus.
A. caudatus, and melancholicus.

The amaranth, or amarantus, is really a cultivated weed—a weed with a college education, as some one has said of the cauliflower as distinguished from common cabbage. The two varieties, *A. caudatus* (Prince's Feather), erect flowering, and *A. melancholicus* (Love-lies-bleeding), with pendulous flower stems, are most common. The flowers in both varieties are generally crimson; both come from India. Another variety, with flowers in an erect blunt spike (*A. hypochondriacus*), is cultivated from Mexico. There is a wretched garden weed of exactly the same figure as the cultivated amarantus, named *A. retroflexus*, commonly called pigweed. Its flowers are green. Celosia, the garden cockscomb, is another near relative of the amarantus; it also comes from India. Its flower crest is generally fan-shaped. These flowers all bloom throughout the summer.

Shrubby St. John's-wort.
Hypericum densiflorum.

St. John's-wort is very common in New Jersey, and it may also be found in more or less plenty north and south of that State. Its flowers are small and golden-yellow, and grow in dense clusters, from which fact it received its botanical name. My drawing is taken from a specimen which grew in the "Pines" of New Jersey. This variety of the flower is a distinctively American one, as *H. perforatum*,

122 FAMILIAR FLOWERS OF FIELD AND GARDEN.

Shrubby St. John's-wort.

which has small and opposite leaves, although commoner in New England, is, as Gray says, "the only one not indigenous." There is no possibility of confusing the two varieties, as one is shrubby and the other has an upright, much-branched stem. The flower gets its name from the superstition that on St. John's day, the 24th of June, the dew which fell on the plant the evening before was efficacious in preserving the eyes from disease. So the plant was collected, dipped in oil, and thus transformed into a balm for every wound. In fact, superstition gathered about the plant in such a variety of forms that the Scotch in olden times carried it about in their pockets as a charm against witchcraft. St. John's-wort can hardly be called beautiful, and it is considered a great nuisance in farming-lands. The shrubby variety grows about three feet high and flowers in June. The *H. perforatum* is an herb which grows one or two feet high and flowers all summer.

Purple-flowering Raspberry.
Rubus odoratus.

The purple-flowering raspberry is not purple at all. This is a popular name without any truth in it. The flowers are crimson-magenta in color, and look something like wild roses; the leaves are somewhat like maple leaves in shape, but are even larger. The fruit looks like a common raspberry, but it is flat, and of a weak red color. There are no thorns on the stems, and, but for this circumstance and the fact that the leaves are so big and strange-looking in the company of the rather striking flower, we might easily mistake it for some kind of a rose. It blooms in June and July.

Purple-flowering Raspberry.

CHAPTER IX.

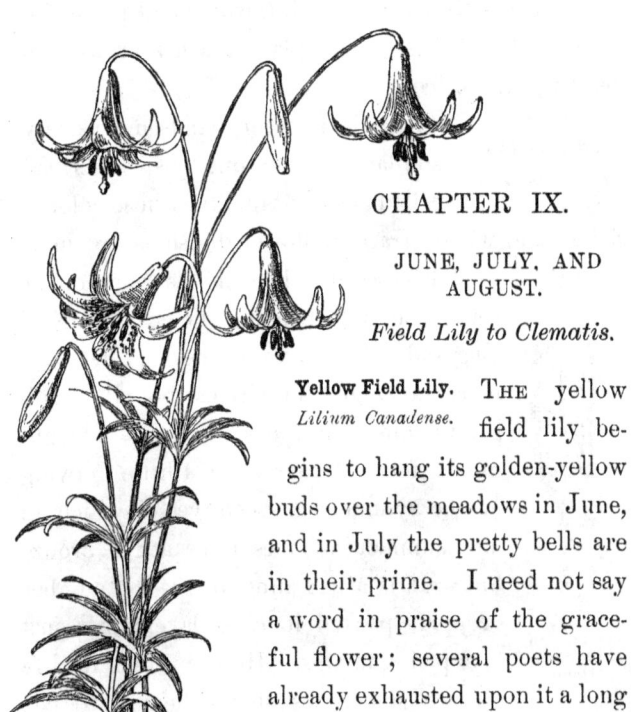

JUNE, JULY, AND AUGUST.

Field Lily to Clematis.

Yellow Field Lily.
Lilium Canadense.

THE yellow field lily begins to hang its golden-yellow buds over the meadows in June, and in July the pretty bells are in their prime. I need not say a word in praise of the graceful flower; several poets have already exhausted upon it a long category of admiring phrases. But we must admit it has a pretty badly freckled face, which perhaps is the reason it hangs its head; however this may be, the graceful droop adds still another charm to the decorative form, and one ought

Lilium Canadense.

to be alone satisfied with such a wonderful perfection of curved outlines. The plant reaches an average height of three feet.

Turk's-cap Lily.
Lilium superbum.

There is another handsome variety, similar to the one just described, called Turk's-cap lily, whose color is richer, and whose graceful flower divisions are more strongly curved backward. This lily is common on Cape Cod and all along the coast of New England. Its leaves are perhaps less regularly arranged in circles, but the stalk grows taller; at times it reaches a height of six feet. I have made a little drawing of the symmetrical seed vessel which in late summer assumes a beautiful bronze hue. It is astonishing to see the number of seeds packed in close layers that just *one* pod contains. How prolific in life Nature sometimes shows herself to be! Each one of those tiny seeds contains a hidden life. Think of the yield of which one *plant* is capable!

Seed-pod of Lilium Superbum.

Wild Red Lily.
Lilium Philadelphicum.

In my estimation the wild red lily, which always grows in shady places (mostly in or on the edge of the woods), is the most beautiful one of all the wild species. Its color is a splendid red of a vermilion cast. The flowers stand erect and resemble tiger lilies turned upward. The stalk grows about two feet high, and generally bears but one flower, orange-yellow outside and vermilion inside, spotted with brown madder — hardly the purple color which Gray mentions. The flower varies in hue, and is sometimes red-orange instead of vermilion. It blooms about the 1st of July, in the thin woods, where the ground is more or less sandy.

Black-eyed Susan.
Rudbeckia hirta.

The black-eyed Susan, as the children call it, Gray says is a Western flower which was introduced into our Eastern meadows with clover seed. It is frequently called cone-flower by reason of the rather high cone-shaped center

Lilium Philadelphicum.

which is usually of a brown-madder color. The flower rays are a rich golden yellow, and have a graceful reflex curve; the flower stems are brownish, stiff, and rough to the touch. The plant grows about eighteen inches high. It blooms in July.

Catchfly.
Silene noctiflora.

The catchfly is common in waste grounds, and is easily identified by its two-parted, white petals. The variety I have sketched is called night-flowering, as the little bud opens only toward evening, or on cloudy days. It blooms side by side with the evening primrose, and might easily be taken for a white variety of the latter flower by one who consults his imagination rather than his botany. But there is really no point of resemblance between the flowers. This catchfly is the most

Rudbeckia Hirta.

beautiful thing imaginable under the magnifying glass; the petals are not so remarkable, but the calyx (the protecting green envelope of the flower) is as delicate as though it were modeled in spun glass; the translucent lines of green and white, the hairy surface, and the symmetry of the tiny form, are all worth the closest examination. My pen-and-ink drawing is hard and coarse beside Nature's perfect art; if the plant had been formed of the most fragile and delicately colored glass it could scarcely have been more curious or beautiful. There are two other varieties of the catchfly which are common: Starry Campion (*Silene stellata*) and Bladder Campion (*Silene inflata*). The petals of the former are cut in a fringe; the stem of the latter is smooth, and its calyx is

Silene Noctiflora.

veined. Gray graphically explains all the minor differences in a way which may be easily understood by one to whom botany is only slightly familiar. The catchfly blooms in early summer.

Field Mouse-ear Chickweed.
Cerastium arvense.

The field mouse-ear chickweed is one of the commonest weeds which grows by our roadsides in all parts of the country. Prof. Meehan says he found it in Bergen Park, Colorado, at a height of seven thousand feet above sea level. So common is the little gray-white flower that my sketch will be all that is needed for its identification. It blooms from April to early August. It has an Alpine origin and does not stand the hot weather well, but with the return of autumn it resumes "a green moss-like growth which it retains through the winter, ready for the early bloom of spring." Thus Prof. Meehan describes its character. The common name has no significance now, as it originated long ago by a fancied resemblance to a certain species of forget-me-not which used to be

Field Mouse-ear Chickweed.

called Mouse-ear, because the leaves resembled in form a mouse's ear. It is not surprising to learn that this flower is a relative of the sandwort (which grows on Mount Washington), and a comparison of my sketches of the two plants will show the close resemblance.

Common Chickweed.
Stellaria media.
Common chickweed is *very* common and troublesome in every garden; it likes damp ground best, and spreads its weakly stems, covered with fine foliage, all over the garden beds. The tiny white flowers are very insignificant; they bloom through spring and summer. *S. longifolia* is another variety with *long* leaves widely spreading, and numerous flowers. *S. borealis* is a variety common northward in all wet, grassy places, and bears its inconspicuous flowers in the forks of the leafy branches. It may be found bordering the springs among the hills of New Hampshire.

Verbena.
Verbena Aubletia.
Our charming garden verbenas are, many of them, indigenous to this country, and may be seen growing wild in Illinois, the Carolinas, and southward. As a rule the flowers are purple. Other garden varieties—pink, red, and white—come from South America, generally the Argentine Republic; one of these (*V. teucroides*) is exceedingly sweet, vanilla-scented. The verbenas flower all summer.

132 FAMILIAR FLOWERS OF FIELD AND GARDEN.

Blue Vervain.
Verbena hastata.

Blue vervain is a tall weed with tiny homely flowers, that grows in waste places and beside the road. There is very little suggestion of blue about it; the flowers are decidedly purple, and so few of them are in bloom at one time that they lack color effect. The plant begins to show its tiny blossoms in July. It is a relative of our beautiful garden verbenas, as its name implies.

Water Arum.
Calla palustris.

The water arum, which is similar in appearance to the cultivated hothouse flower called calla lily (wrongly named, as it does not belong to the Lily family), is common in boggy places north of Pennsylvania. It flowers in early summer, and is certainly pretty enough to deserve cultivation; but its magnificent relative, so much superior in size, evidently precludes the probability of the horticulturist taking interest in the lesser flower. It seems a pity, for the wild calla is

Blue Vervain.

very beautiful, but not quite so common as we might wish; we have to look for it. Thoreau says, after finding this calla in a certain locality near Concord: "Having found this in one place, I now find it in another. Many an object is not seen, though it falls within the range of our visual ray, because it does not come within the range of our intellectual ray. So in the largest sense we find only the world we look for." This is in a great measure true regarding a search for certain wild flowers. They are only to be seen on demand!

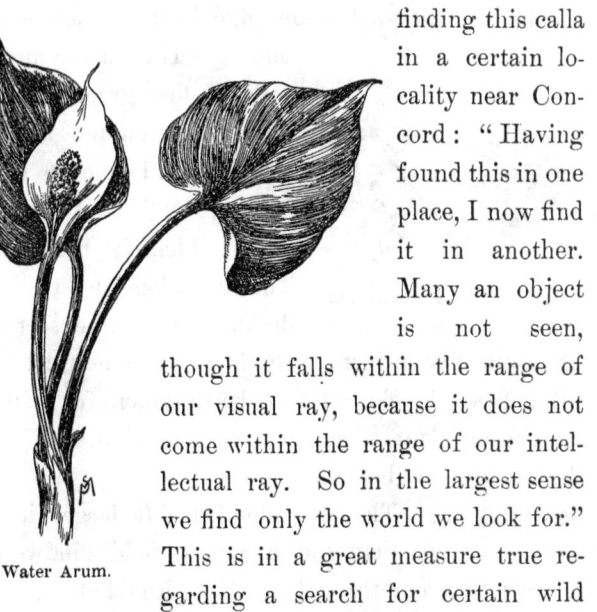

Water Arum.

Wild Sarsaparilla. The wild sarsaparilla, which must
Aralia nudicaulis. not be mistaken for the true sarsaparilla of soda-water fame, is nevertheless often used as a substitute for the officinal article. Its slender roots, which run horizontally three or four feet in every direction away from the stem, are as aromatic as the mucilaginous twigs of the sassafras tree. But every country boy knows all about sassafras and

sarsaparilla ; any plant which appeals to his sense of taste or his propensity to chew is a component part of the well-digested knowledge he never learned at school. The rather pretty balls of fine greenish-white flowers of unique appearance, which bloom in early summer, will easily enable one to identify the plant. The single long-stalked leaf, divided into three sections of about five leaflets each, is too symmetrical and pronounced in character to be mistaken for that of any other plant when the peculiar globes of tiny flowers are seen below it.

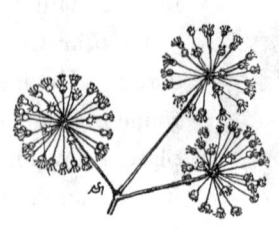

Flowers of Wild Sarsaparilla.

Hedge Bindweed. The hedge bindweed (a larger flower
Calystegia sepium. than the European field bindweed), is very common throughout New England. In appearance the flower is exactly like a pinky-white garden morning-glory, to which it is closely related; but the leaf is quite different; it is not heart-shaped, but looks more like an arrowhead. The pretty vine climbs over the hedges beside the road, and covers the unsightly brushwood with a glory of dainty white flower bells, whose delicate pink flush is unequaled by the tint of many a highly cultivated garden flower. But the bindweed is a

dangerous character to bring into the garden; it is apt to choke everything it can get hold of, and it spreads with remarkable rapidity from year to year. The flowers begin to bloom in July. Our garden morning-glory (*Ipomœa purpurea*), with a heart-shaped leaf, comes from South America.

Dodder. That most distressing weed which goes
Cuscuta Gronovii. by the name of dodder is a plague which, in its disintegrating power, can only be compared to sin! It works the greatest mischief if it gets within the confines of the garden. The little vine is parasitic, and it saps the energy of every plant it can fasten itself upon! Celia Thaxter evidently had great trouble with it in her island garden. She speaks of it thus: "The plants emerge from the ground, each like a fine yellow hair, till they are an inch and a half or two inches long; they reach with might and main toward the nearest legitimate-growing plant, and when they touch it, cling like a limpet; then they draw their other end up out of the ground and set up housekeeping for the rest of their lives. They adhere to the unhappy individual upon which they have fixed themselves with a grip that grows more and more horrible; they suck all its juices, drink all its health and strength and beauty, and fling out trailers to the next, and the next, and the next, till the whole garden is a mass of ruin and despair."

The slender wiry stems are light yellow-brown in color, and are destitute of leaves; the flowers are dull white little things which grow in clusters at intervals on the twining stalk. Down East the weed grows in wet places, and covers shrubs and plants with a tangled mass of amber-colored threads which produce a rather pretty effect among the green. It flowers in early summer. It is a near relative of the morning-glory.

Bedstraw. The little vine called *Galium triflorum.* bedstraw has an interesting conventional leaf, but an inconspicuous white flower much less effective than sweet alyssum. The sweet-scented variety is common in the glades of the White Hills and in the thickets which border the rivers there. The flowers have, in my opinion, a sickening-sweet odor which is unpleasant. The vine is a pretty little thing, whose circularly arranged leaves give it a decorative look. The most extraordinary thing about bedstraw is the way it catches on everything it touches; the microscope will tell the reason why. In my frequent walks to a secluded spot on the brink of the beautiful Pemigewasset

Galium.

River, where one may indulge in a refreshing bath on a hot July day, I pass through a belt of shrubbery so thick with bedstraw that the odor is overpowering, and advance is checked by the sticky vine which at every point catches on one's clothing.

Poison Ivy.
Rhus Toxicodendron.
On the meadows which border the same river will be seen, all through the summer, the drooping three-leafed vine called poison ivy, or mercury. Gray says it is a vile pest, and I perfectly agree with his estimate of its character. It poisons some people dreadfully. Although I had many a time touched the leaves with my *fingers* without experiencing any ill effect, at last came a miserable experience : a bit of the wretched plant came in contact with the more sensitive skin, which is very different from the callous cuticle of the finger-tips, and the poison began to act like fire a few days afterward; nothing but cloths saturated with Pond's Extract (witch-hazel) seemed to be of any use in alleviating the burning, itching sensation. But some persons are poisoned by even *passing* through a district where the ivy grows; so it is best to avoid it altogether. Curiously enough, an extract of *Rhus Toxicodendron* is a homœopathic specific for skin diseases. It has a very smooth, fresh green leaf, with an unvarnished surface, which always occurs in threes, and therefore should not be mistaken for the Virginia

creeper (*Ampelopsis quinquefolia*), which is a five-leafed vine. In the hills of New Hampshire the cold winters prevent any woody growth of the poison ivy, and the vine trails at one's feet over meadow and roadside; but near Boston I have seen stone walls covered with the woody branches which had attained a tall and shrublike appearance. In autumn the clusters of small gray berries are rather decorative, and the leaves turn a pretty red. I have more than once found the witch-hazel (*Hamamelis Virginica*) growing side by side with the ivy.

Clematis, or Virgin's Bower.
Clematis Virginiana.

The beautiful clematis vine hangs in festoons from the trees, and covers the stone walls beside the roads which follow the river courses among the hills of New Hampshire. For that matter it grows everywhere, and is quite as common in the Berkshire country and in the vicinity of northern New Jersey. The little flower has four greenish-white sepals which look like petals, and a great number of stamens; it grows in beautiful, graceful clusters. In the fall the gray plumes of the flowers gone to seed are very striking, and the hoary appearance of the vine at this season suggested the name old man's beard. The vine supports itself by a twist in the leaf stem; it is curious to note the turn of these stems, which actually revolve in as short a space of time as the tips of

JUNE, JULY, AND AUGUST. 139

the morning-glory vine. Certainly clematis is one of the most lovely vines which grow wild on our country highways and by-ways; in August it is covered with dainty clusters of starry blossoms, and in October it is arrayed in the silver gray of its plumed seed vessels. It will bear transplanting, and flourishes in the coldest climate. Nothing is prettier than its graceful branches decorating a rustic fence. It flowers in midsummer. Mme. Edouard Andre is a new variety of the vine in cultivation with handsome reddish flowers. *C. graveolens* is a variety cultivated from Thibet with yellow flowers. *C. paniculata* is a beautiful

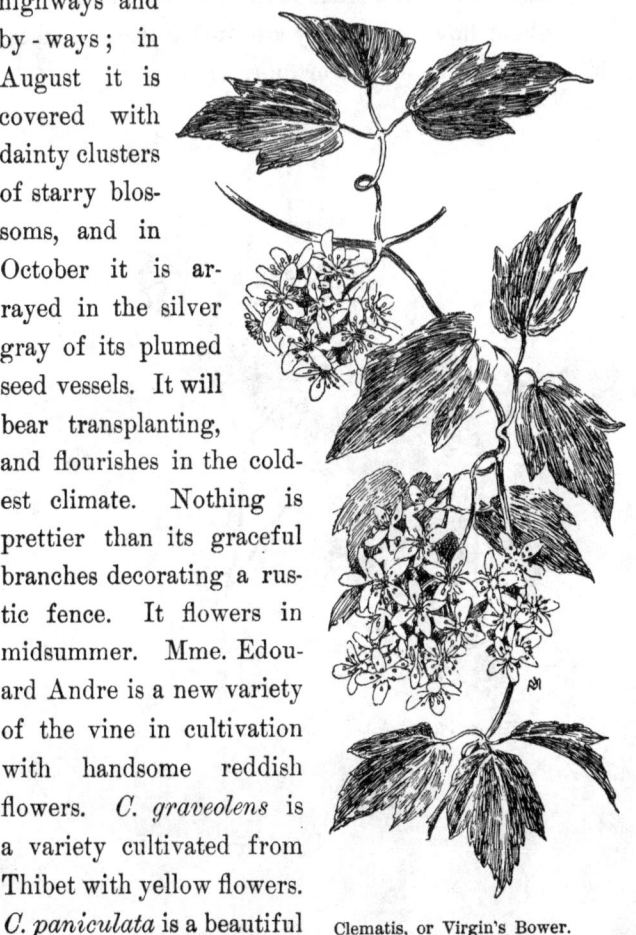

Clematis, or Virgin's Bower.

species in cultivation, with flowers somewhat similar in appearance to the wild variety, but more luxuriant in growth; it comes from Japan. *C. Jackmanni* is a violet-blue flowered variety also in cultivation, whose blossoms are two inches or more broad.

Hoary Plume of the Clematis, or Old Man's Beard.

CHAPTER X.

JUNE TO OCTOBER.

Poppy to Love-in-a-Mist.

The Poppy. THE Poppy family is so large and so
Papaver. varied in type that a garden filled
with all the different varieties would present an astonishing picture of contrasting forms and colors from the 1st of June until the middle of October. Yet, notwithstanding this fact, there are few who allow the family a fair representation in their gardens. Our knowledge of poppies, therefore, is generally confined to a very few varieties.

Gray says we have no truly wild species; all our poppies come from the Old World; but he mentions a variety (*P. dubium*) which has run wild in fields in Pennsylvania. In England and Scotland, and even in Italy, the graceful, single, scarlet poppy is commonly seen growing wild, especially in fields where wheat is sown. I have gathered quantities of the flowers in waste places within the walls of Rome. It seems strange that this easy-growing annual has not obtained the same strong foothold in our own country. For six years I have picked strong and healthy poppies in a certain part of my garden, where, after the first sowing, the seed has taken the matter into its own hands; but the flower has not yet consented to the degenerate estate of a weed like its European companions—toadflax, chicory, viper's bugloss, and tansy.

The classification of poppies in the seedsmen's catalogues is somewhat confusing; as a rule, they present three divisions—Ranunculus, Pæony, and Carnation. The two last-mentioned varieties may be included under the general name which Gray uses, *P. somniferum*, or opium poppy. The first-mentioned variety may be included under Gray's name, *P. Rhœas*, or corn poppy, of Europe. There is also a perennial variety, called *P. orientale*, or Oriental poppy, which is mentioned by the seedsmen as well as by Gray. Under these three names we may include *all* the commoner varieties of poppies which we may find in the garden.

The less common varieties are *P. nudicaule*, or Iceland poppy (perennial); *P. glaucium*, or tulip poppy; and the more distant family connections, *Argemone Mexicana*, or prickly poppy, and *Eschscholtzia Californica*, or California poppy. I might add that our *Sanguinaria Canadensis*, or blood-root, is a near relative of the poppy.

The seedsmen use the names Ranunculus, Pæony, and Carnation merely to distinguish the types of certain flowers; thus, one flower bears a resemblance to the garden ranunculus, another to the pæony, and another to the carnation. That these types are very distinct, an examination of the petals will abundantly prove. My drawing of the poppy called Rosy Morn is an example of a pæony-shaped flower; the daintier Mikado and Fairy Blush are examples of carnation-shaped flowers. The Shirley and the Double French poppies belong to the Ranunculus division.

The poppy is an extraordinarily beautiful flower; it would be partial for me to recommend any particular variety; but if I were asked which one seemed to be the most beautiful, I think I should be

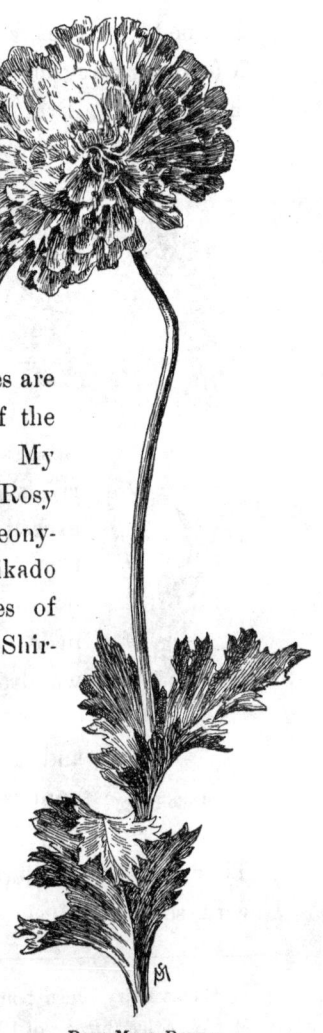

Rosy Morn Poppy.

inclined to answer, Fairy Blush; but then would come a feeling of regret at the injustice done Rosy Morn, Eider Down, Bride, and New Cardinal. Still, the Fairy Blush is a most perfect beauty, whose creamy white delicately penciled with the purest strong pink is transcendently lovely. I have grown specimens in my garden which measured four inches across.* The Rosy Morn grows even larger, and possesses a wealth of warm pink which rivals many a rose. But I could not exceed Celia Thaxter in her admiration for the glorious poppy, and I can not do better than quote what she says in An Island Garden: "I think for wondrous variety, for certain picturesque qualities, for color and form, and a subtile mystery of character, poppies seem . . . the most satisfactory flowers among the annuals. . . . They are the tenderest lilac, richest scarlet, white with softest suffusion of rose—all shades of rose—

Mikado Poppy.

---

* This Fairy Blush poppy was raised from seed obtained from Mr. W. Atlee Burpee, of Philadelphia.

clear light pink with sea-green center, the anthers in a golden halo about it; black and fire-color; red that is deepened into black, with gray reflections, cherry-color with a cross of creamy white at the bottom of the cup, and round its central altar of ineffable golden green again the halo of yellow anthers. . . . Oh, these white poppies, some with petals more delicate than the finest tissue paper, with centers of bright gold, some of thicker quality, large shell-like petals, almost ribbed in their effect, their green knob in the middle like a boss upon a shield, rayed about with beautiful grayish-yellow stamens, as in the kind called the Bride. Others—they call this kind the Snowdrift—have thick double flowers, deeply cut and fringed at the edges, the most opaque white, and full of exquisite shadows. Then there are the Icelanders, which Lieutenant Peary found making gay the frosty fields of Greenland, in buttercup-yellow and orange and white; the great Orientals, gorgeous beyond expression; and the im-

Shirley Poppy.

mense single white California variety. . . . As for the Shirleys, they are children of the dawn, and inherit all its delicate, vivid, delicious suffusions of rose-color in every conceivable shade. The Thorn Poppy (*Argemone*) is a fascinating variety, most quaint in method of growth and most decorative."

It seems as though there was nothing left to say about the color of poppies after this; yet we see the Fairy Blush and the New Cardinal are not mentioned! So great is the variety of individual types that it would be nearly impossible for one to become well acquainted with them all. Some specimens of the pretty little globe-shaped variety, called Japanese Pompon, look as if they were spun from the most delicate, soft China silk. The single Shirley is a variety from which every bit of black blood has been eliminated; so they possess the daintiest and palest tints. The Iceland poppies are glorious in yellow and orange, and Umbrosum is a rich scarlet with a black cross at the base. Argemone (a Mexican variety) is a dainty white flower with a golden center, and the most delicate transparent flower

Ranunculus poppy, seed pod.

Pæony poppy seed pod.

I can think of is the semi-double white poppy belonging to the Ranunculus division; this is as fair as the daintiest wild rose.

The character of the foliage in the two divisions, Ranunculus and Pæony (carnation is the same with the pæony), is entirely different. The leaves of the former variety are grass-green and round-edged; the leaves of the latter clasp the stem, are a light cabbage-green, smooth, with sharp-pointed edges, and have an extremely decorative form, not unlike the famous acanthus leaf which furnished inspiration to the Greek artists in the designing of the most beautiful capital for a column the world has ever seen.

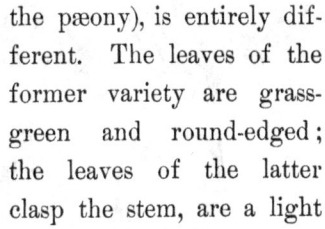

Flag of Truce Poppy.

The opium poppy, which is cultivated in India and Persia, has white petals and white seeds; I consider the single flower, called Flag of Truce, typical of this variety. The opium poppy cultivated in Asia Minor has purplish flowers and black seeds.

The charming California poppy receives its name from a German naturalist by the name of Eschscholtz; it possesses the most brilliant and perfect yellow and orange in existence. No flower can equal it in color, and the artist's paint box contains no pigment which can approach it within "hailing distance." It has a range of bright hues from pure yellow to deep orange, and a cream-yellow white which is exceedingly soft and beautiful. The peculiar little pointed calyx rests extinguisher-like on the flaming yellow petals, and is forced off whole as the flower expands. Although the flower is common in California and grows there in great abundance as a wild flower without value, it is prized very highly in the East as a garden annual.

Eschscholtzia.

The tree poppy (*Dendromecon rigidum*) of California is six or eight feet high and bears brilliant yellow flowers, not unlike *Eschscholtzia*, nearly three inches broad. This is remarkable as a shrubby plant belonging to an almost wholly herbaceous family, the *Papaveraceæ*.

The poppy is extensively employed in the conventional ornament of India, and one of the most beautiful finial ornaments in Gothic architecture is called the poppy-head.

Argemone is not as familiar an object in the garden as one might wish. The variety called *Albiflora* is the only one commonly cultivated; this has large white flowers with yellow anthers. The yellow variety produces pretty flowers not as brilliant in color as *Eschscholtzia*, and therefore less frequently met with in the garden. But the pity of it is that poppies are such ephemeral characters. Burns says very truly in Tam o' Shanter:

> "But pleasures are like poppies spread,
> You seize the flower, its bloom is shed."

Pot Marigold.
Calendula officinalis.

The pot marigold, or calendula, is a common garden flower which, in my estimation, is not half appreciated. The name calendula is suggestive; it comes from the Latin *calendæ*, first day of the month. It is a fact that the calendula will bloom through each month. It has a most extraordinary power of supply, and from July until late in November, if it is protected from frost, it will continue to bloom with unabating vigor. It will also bloom in the greenhouse all winter and through the following spring.

Its orange and yellow are superb and vie with the

magnificent hues of the *Eschscholtzia;* nothing can surpass the royal color of the Prince of Orange, and no yellow is purer and stronger than that of the lemon or sulphur calendula. The Meteor is beautifully striped with pumpkin-orange on a yellow ground, and Trianon is a bright-yellow flower with a brown boss in the center. My favorite variety is the pale-tinted Le Proust, which has a dark center and a circle of closely packed, light yellow-buff rays. Like the nasturtium, the calendula produces an unlimited supply of flowers on the condition that the blossoms must be continually picked.

Le Proust Calendula.

It is a pity that the plant is generally considered an ill-scented one; even Gray mentions this little drawback. But I like the smell of calendulas; it is herby and grateful—at least to *my* olfactory nerves. Perhaps this may be on account of a long-continued acquaintance with the flower, but it is a significant fact that those who really love Nature's beautiful things take few exceptions to her peculiarities, and I will admit that the smell of the calendula is peculiar.

However, if we choose, we may easily cultivate a catholicity of taste which at least will exempt us from the danger of one which is prudish. The English use the calendula to flavor their soups, and the leaves are also boiled down in fat for use as a healing salve. The term officinal, it might be well to mention just here, is applied to plants which have a commercial value, and are commonly on sale. As a rule, many plants have officinal roots; this is the case with the true sarsaparilla and licorice (*Glycyrrhiza glabra*). But the calendula is more beautiful than it is useful, and the double varieties are extremely ornamental in the garden; the petals, or rather corollas, are compactly fitted together, and are strap-shaped and resemble the close-fitting little feathers on the neck of a bird. What we call the seed of the flower—which is a dry, green, rough, curled-up little thing less than half an inch in length, with a general resemblance to a small green worm—is, botanically speaking, an akene or small, dry, one-seeded fruit which is usually mistaken for a naked seed. But the akene is evidently more than the seed; it includes the ripened pistil of the flower, and upon cutting it open the seed, with its shell, is found complete within. The akenes of the calendula all belong to the ray flowers; the disk flowers are sterile. In the immense Composite family of which the calendula is a member, all the so-

152 FAMILIAR FLOWERS OF FIELD AND GARDEN.

called seeds are akenes. A naked seed is instanced by that of the portulaca in the Purslane family, where we will find it carefully tucked away with many companions in a tiny box with a lid.

Gaillardia, or Blanket Flower.
Gaillardia pulchella.

In the Gaillardia of our gardens we really have a cultivated flower which is our own—a native of our country. It originally came from Louisiana, and was first brought into France by M. Thouin, a professor of agriculture in Paris, in 1787. The plant was named for a M. Gaillardet, who was a patron of botany. It is a pretty flower in its single form, slightly resembling coreopsis, but is more highly colored than the latter flower; its hues are varied in reds and deep and pale yellows. There is a handsome double variety named *G. Lorenziana*, whose flowers are mixed yellow and flame-color, and somewhat resemble small chrysanthemums. But I fancy the single varieties more. It is frequently the case that a beautiful single flower gains little or nothing by the doubling process. The charming *G. amblyodon*, of

Gaillardia.

a blood-red color, is now cultivated in our gardens, and is a native of Texas, where it grows in profusion on the banks of the Brazos. Another beautiful cultivated variety is Aurora Borealis, whose colors are gold, rich red, and white. *G. aristata* grows wild in Missouri and farther west, and has also come under cultivation. Its showy rays are either yellow throughout or are dashed with brownish purple at their base. *G. lanceolata* grows wild southward from Carolina, in the pine barrens, has narrow leaves, and flower heads with small yellow rays and brownish-purple disks. The Gaillardias are both perennials and annuals; the varieties *G. amblyodon* and *G. pulchella* are annuals. All are summer flowering plants.

Summer Chrysanthemum.
Chrysanthemum coronarium.

The summer chrysanthemum is a charming annual held in high esteem by the farmers' wives, particularly in New England. In nearly every dooryard, where there are any flowers at all, we will be pretty sure to see in summer the *Coronarium chrysanthemum*. The

Summer Chrysanthemum, Burridgeanum.

single varieties I do not fancy; they are artificial-looking, but withal rather decorative. The double flowers are splendid in golden yellow and yellowish white, and the plants bloom with prodigal liberality. Of the single varieties I consider *Burridgeanum*, which is white with a crimson band and yellow toward the center, the most attractive.

Love-in-a-Mist. Love-in-a-mist is *Nigella Damascena.* a peculiar character with wiry or misty foliage—whichever you please to call it—and white or pale violet-white flowers which curiously nestle beneath the fine foliage. It is rather a strange than a beautiful flower, but it deserves a place in the garden for variety's sake. It blooms throughout the summer, and is an annual which has long been a favorite with those who have a taste for the old-fashioned.

Love-in a-Mist.

CHAPTER XI.

JUNE, JULY, AUGUST, AND SEPTEMBER.

Loosestrife to Jewelweed.

Four-leaved Loosestrife.
Lysimachia quadrifolia.

Four-leaved loosestrife, as distinguished from the other common variety, which is called yellow loosestrife, may be identified by its leaves, which generally grow in fours on the stem at regular intervals. The pretty little golden-yellow, star-shaped flowers, with a touch of rusty color between each point, grow out on a rather long, fine stem from the point where the leaf joins the main stalk. This loosestrife grows thick at the

Four-leaved Loosestrife.

edge of the thickets which border the meadows of Campton, N. H. It is not a striking flower, but it attracts one by its tiny symmetry and pretty yellow color. It blooms in early summer, and flourishes where the soil is sandy. There is a purple loosestrife (*Lythrum Salicaria*) which blooms in August, and is not quite so common as the yellow varieties. Its flowers are magenta, and the narrow petals are curved and twisted; the leaves are lance-shaped. It grows in wet ground.

Common Loosestrife. The common loosestrife grows in
Lysimachia stricta. low, wet ground, and may easily be distinguished from the four-leaved variety by its branching habit and its flower cluster which terminates the stem; it is also more leafy. The color effect of this flower, growing thickly beneath the scattered groups of low birch and elder-berry which dot the intervales in the White Mountain region, is very beautiful. The yellow color blends softly with the shadowy green of the foliage in July. I remember no prettier sight than a long belt of loosestrife which skirts the shrubbery surrounding a retreat to which the boys resort on the warm July days—the popular bathing place. Loosestrife may be found almost anywhere; not only with the environment just described, but on the banks of the beautiful rivers which wind through the Vermont hills, in the

valley of the Hudson, beside the streams which flow through the Catskills, and in the immediate vicinity of Boston. It is interesting to know that the dainty, white star-flower is closely related to loose-strife. They both belong to the Primrose family.

Turtle-head. The turtle-head
Chelone glabra. may be found with the same surroundings as the loosestrife, or perhaps down close by the river. It is a reserved character, and in this respect resembles the closed gentian in having a shut-up look! Its flowers are white or pinkish, and bloom in August. It is a relative of the garden snap dragon. My sketch will be sufficient for its identification.

Turtle-head.

Tall Meadow-Rue.
Thalictrum Cornuti.

The beautiful tall meadow-rue begins to show its plumes of feathery white flowers in early summer when the yellow field lily is in full bloom. I call to mind a lovely spot on the meadows of Campton, N. H., where the graceful lilies hang their score of golden bells against a shady background of low birch which is lighted up here and there by the soft, white bloom of the tall meadow-rue; such a picture one can not forget; and the sleepy heat of a July day, the hum of insects, the buzz of a lazy bumblebee, and the rustling of tall grass disturbed by the flight of a ground sparrow — these are all the living parts of a picture in which the meadow-rue's tall and graceful figure stands supreme. The ornamental blue-green leaves are well worth close study, as they are charm-

Tall Meadow-Rue.

ingly decorative; it is also interesting to notice how like they are to the leaves of the *Anemonella thalictroides*.

Early Meadow-Rue. There is another quite common
Thalictrum dioicum. meadow-rue (*T. dioicum*) which, it seems to me, ought to be called *wood* rue, as it nearly always grows on the borders of the forest. This variety is about eighteen inches tall, and bears insignificant brownish-green flowers which fail to attract one when they appear in late spring.

Thorn-Apple. The thorn-apple, so called on ac-
Datura Stramonium. count of its round, green, thorny fruit, is one of the rankest-smelling weeds in existence. It is only necessary for one to crush a leaf or stem between the fingers to be thoroughly assured of the fact that the weed is *repulsively* rank—not attractively rank like the onion. Memory recalls a certain empty lot next to the house in which I lived in Brooklyn where there was a rubbish

Thorn-Apple Blossom.

heap pretty well ornamented with this white-flowered *Datura*. I transplanted some of the weed in my garden, and was ridiculed for the bad taste displayed in liking such a rank thing; but the flowers were beautiful to my boyish eyes, and *now* the magnificent *D. cornucopia*, which is but a recent highly cultivated variety of the same flower, is greatly sought after by those who wish to ornament their gardens. The flower has a long, tubular five-pointed corolla set in a long, light-green calyx. It blooms in early summer, and is a familiar object in open lots around New York and the cities of northern New Jersey. I never found it in New Hampshire.

Spreading Dogbane.
Apocynum androsæmifolium.

The spreading dogbane is so common all over the country in thickets and woody dells that one can not fail to find it without the effort of a regular search. It is easy to identify the small, loose clusters of tiny, pinky-white, bell-shaped flowers which resemble lilies-of-the-valley, and grow on a bush that bears smallish, oval, dull, light-green leaves; on breaking off a stem it exudes a sticky milk-white juice, as the milkweed does. The flowers are quite as beautiful as many small garden favorites, and in my estimation they are individually more attractive by reason of their delicious dainty pink flush than the lily-of-the-valley. This seems flat heresy, but in defense of the preference for a common wild flower I would venture to predict that if some horticulturist should succeed in producing a lily-of-the-valley with the dainty pink coloring of the dogbane,

JUNE, JULY, AUGUST, AND SEPTEMBER. 161

such a flower with its charming perfume would be wildly admired by every lover of flowers. Such is the disadvantage of the wild flower that its beauty is discounted if it has not reached an abnormal devel-

Spreading Dogbane.

opment, and its charms are unheeded if it does not throw out a perfume strong enough to entice the passer-by. The dogbane blooms in early summer, and it is often found in the company of the milkweed.

Common Milkweed. The com-
Asclepias Cornuti. mon milkweed needs no introduction; its pretty pods of white silk are familiar to every child, who treasures them until the time comes when the place in which they are stowed away is one mass of bewildering, unmanageable white fluff. Then there are vague talks about stuffing pillows and all that sort of thing; but the first attempt to manipulate the lawless, airy down usually results in disastrous confusion, and whole

Milkweed Down.

masses go floating away on the slightest zephyr. Of course, there is more fun in chasing milkweed down than in patiently stuffing a pillow; so the milkweed has its own way and goes sailing off to scatter its seeds hither and thither, and the pillow, perhaps, is filled with the aromatic balsam fir. But, before the last tiny tuft of silk has escaped with its balancing brown seed, we must place it under the microscope and examine the bronze-colored seed and the strange downy sail. Can one imagine anything more perfect? Place some bits of white sewing silk beside the sheeny silk of Nature, and the former will look like coarse, white rope. Gray must have been puzzled to know how to describe the color of the milkweed's flowers; what a predicament for Nature to put a color-blind botanist in! She has evidently mixed up all the colors on her palette and painted the beautiful blossoms in absolutely neutral tints. Gray does not stop to analyze the color, but dismisses the matter by labeling the flower "dull greenish purplish." Now, if we will take the paint box and mix pure green and pure purple together, and then throw in a tiny bit of black to get the "dull" effect, we will not approach the color of the milkweed's flower. No, Nature did not produce her color that way; the flower is neither green nor purple, nor a mixture of those colors, but is a neutralized *brown*, so we must call it brown, with modifications which fit the case. My modification, then, would be pale *lavender* brown, with a few touches of pale-brown lavender. For the indorsement of my statement I must refer to the microscope; under it the colors will show themselves definitely, and the flower will also prove to be exquisitely formed. The milkweed is in blossom during the early part of the summer; its heavy perfume is cloying; in other words, it is altogether *too* sweet.

Milkweed.

Butterfly Weed. The butterfly weed is a variety of
Asclepias tuberosa. milkweed which is very common through New England, particularly in the vicinity of Cape Cod. It grows in dry sandy places, blooms in midsummer, and stains the pastures with a brilliant orange-color, which, I should think, would set a colorist of the impressionist school quite wild. The shape of the flowers is almost exactly like that of the

Floating Seed of Butterfly Weed.

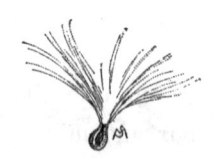

common milkweed; but, unlike the latter plant, the stems and stalks when broken do not exude a plentiful supply of sticky "milk." I have drawn the seed pod, which is slenderer than that of common milkweed, and more interesting; it bursts later, and holds on its ragged-looking contents better, thus giving the dried and shriveled plant a weird appearance, suggestive of a wild, gray-haired witch.

Harebell.
Campanula rotundifolia.

The dainty harebell, which looks so frail that it seems as though a cold gust of wind might wither its transparent blue and break its delicate stem, is one of the hardiest of all our smaller wild flowers. This flower is, in fact, no other than the rugged bluebell of Scotland. It will be found blooming in the meadows in early June, and northward it can be gathered on the mountain tops as late as September. I have found perfect specimens on the slopes of Mount Washington and on the edges of the rocky cliffs which flank the southern side of Mount Willard, in the Crawford Notch, as late as the 20th of September. The pretty little blue, pointed bells can be often seen hanging over a precipice and swinging at every passing breeze with a fearlessness which one would expect in a larger flower with a bolder aspect. But goats and bluebells are

Seed pod of the Butterfly Weed.

quite at home on rocky precipices, and it would take more than a cyclone to disturb the sure footing of either. I have seen a little plant, eight inches high, bend its wiry stem prone beneath the blast, and yet the half dozen flower bells it held were not broken off nor injured. Those of us whose gardens have been visited by the sudden gale which will sometimes precede a thunderstorm know what sad havoc it works among flowers which have every appearance of strength. But it is the stout oak which falls with a crash in a high wind which only bends the supple reed. The harebell was built to stand the mountain storm. The flower has a beautiful purple color, scarcely approaching blue; this color is so charmingly graduated within the bell that in its

Harebell.

depths it is misty-looking. The color of the anthers and the stamens, five in number, are surprisingly pretty when viewed through a magnifying glass; the stems and leaves are wiry and tough; but the tenderer round leaf, from which the plant gets its botanical name, springs directly from the root and dies early.

Self-heal. The very famil-
Brunella vulgaris. iar rusty-green heads of this small blue (more correctly blue-purple) flower called self-heal are ever present beside the road and on the edge of the pasture. All summer long the tireless little flower blossoms almost anywhere we may happen to look. It is provoking to see a common thing so constantly and yet not to know its name; and I venture to say there are but few of us who recognize

Brunella.

it as *Brunella*. But one can claim only a scraping acquaintance with a flower who knows it by sight and by name; *Brunella*, I think, deserves more attention. If a good specimen is placed under the microscope, it will reveal quite a pretty little face. We can not see its perfect form without the glass; the upper part is hooded over, and the lower has a flange on either side and a lip below which seem to invite the passing bumblebee to step in and take a sip of honey. There is pretty nearly always a yellow-striped visitor hanging on one of these purple flowers of the self-heal; his head is buried up to his ears in the tiny corolla, and we must shake him off if we wish to get a close view of the pretty little stamens and pistil which are encircled by the miniature, soft purple throat. The flower is in bloom from June to October.

Common Meadow-Sweet.
Spiræa salicifolia.

The common meadow-sweet is common enough in some places, but rare in others. I have never found it in the southern Catskills nor in the northern part of New Jersey, although I dare say it grows in both localities. In my estimation, a flower is common when you see it without the slight exertion of looking for it. I have never *looked* for the flower in the localities mentioned; but experiences differ, and some people are fortunate in finding things which are not common, in very common places. One does not need to *look* for the soft plumes of the meadow-sweet in the moist nooks of the highways among the White Hills during the early summer; they are before one's eyes everywhere. Damp ground or dry, it is all the same; there is the pretty bush with its plume of pinkish-white flowers directly before us. I find it, too, quite as common in the Berkshire country; and Dora Read Goodale says:

> ". . . she follows every turn
> With spires of closely clustered bloom,
> And all the wildness of the place,
> The narrow pass, the rugged ways,
> But give her larger room.
>
> "And near the unfrequented road,
> By waysides scorched with barren heat,
> In clouded pink or softer white
> She holds the summer's generous light—
> Our native meadow-sweet!"

But it was a New England girl who wrote this, and very true it is so far as New England is concerned; but look for the flower in the vicinity of Lake George, and the poetry does not apply.

Hardhack, or Steeple Bush. *Spiræa tomentosa.* Hardhack, or steeple bush, is another *Spiræa* just a little different from meadow-sweet. The flowers are pinker, the plume is perpendicular and sharp-pointed, the under side of the leaves and also the brown stems are cottony-looking, and the terminal bloom is more apt to look brown and faded below and fresh above. Gray says the flowers are rose-purple in color; this is not correct, as the term rose-purple is anomalous; rose-color (if one may be permitted to repeat so indefinite a term) is usually pure pink, and pink is removed from a purplish tint by an unavoidably intermediate crimson one. So Gray evidently means magenta-pink. But the flowers are not this color; they vary in a range of pink between the vermilion kind and the crimson kind. I am absolutely explicit in thus naming the color; the pink never approaches purple nearer than the crimson point. One glance at the tiny hawthornlike flowers through the magnifying glass is a wonderful revelation : we involuntarily express some surprise that Nature should take so much pains about the detail of such a tiny thing; what a waste of

Hardhack.

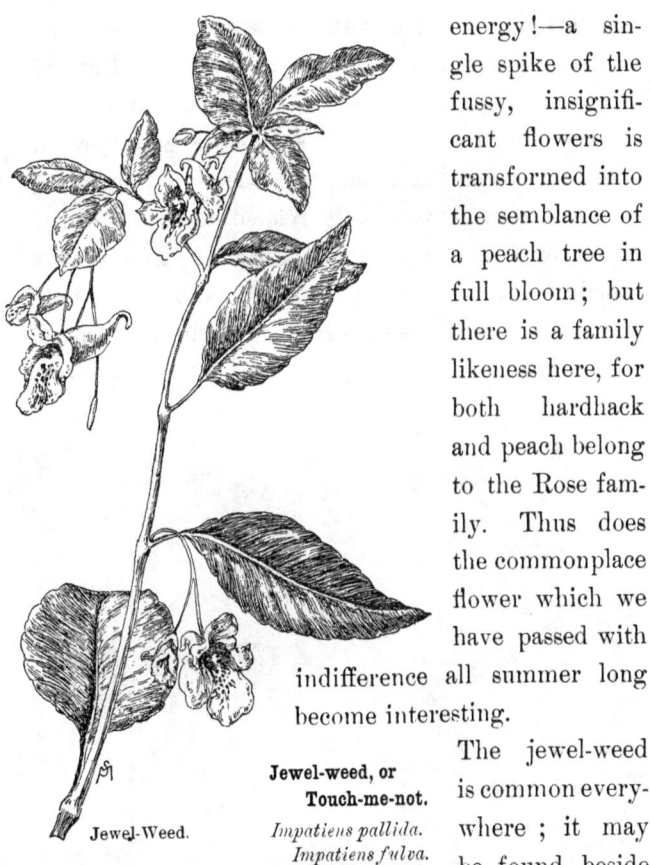

energy!—a single spike of the fussy, insignificant flowers is transformed into the semblance of a peach tree in full bloom; but there is a family likeness here, for both hardhack and peach belong to the Rose family. Thus does the commonplace flower which we have passed with indifference all summer long become interesting.

Jewel-Weed.

Jewel-weed, or Touch-me-not.
Impatiens pallida.
Impatiens fulva.

The jewel-weed is common everywhere; it may be found beside the horse trough, or overhanging the spring, or in some shady dell where a tiny stream flows sluggishly along through the soft ground. The weed frequently has some bedstraw clinging to it, and it is always associated in my mind with the latter sweet-smelling vine, whose perfume is like sweet alyssum. But the flower of the jewel-weed is scentless, and is only pretty in color, which is a spotty orange-yellow; it is so like the garden balsam that one is not surprised to learn that it is closely related to this favorite flower of our grandmothers' gardens. The variety called *I. fulva* is common South, and has deeper-colored flowers. Both varieties bloom all through the summer.

CHAPTER XII.

JULY TO OCTOBER.

Toadflax to Bouncing Bet.

Toadflax, or Butter and Eggs.
Linaria vulgaris.

TOADFLAX is another pretty wild flower which is common everywhere, in the field and beside the road. The children's name for it, butter and eggs, so far as colors are concerned, is remarkably appropriate; the blossom has an egg-orange-colored protuberance in the center with pale butter-colored flanges above and below. A full spike of the flower is very symmetrical, and a quantity of them closely grouped is a pretty sight indeed. The flowers have a cheery look,

Toadflax.

like the flock of daffodils on the margin of the lake which Wordsworth sang about; but no one of our poets sings the praises of butter and eggs, and their dainty coloring brightens the dullness of waste places beside our highways in vain—yet not quite in vain, for the flower is a great favorite among the children. It is very common in the Catskills, but rather rare in the heart of the White Mountains. It decorates every empty city lot, and yet it is not a native of our country, but was brought here from Europe. It is in bloom from July until late October.

Wild Blue Toadflax. There is another, blue-colored wild
Linaria Canadensis. toadflax, common in the Middle States though rarely found down East, which is not nearly so pretty as its orange and yellow relative. It is pale blue-purple in color, has a rather scrawny flower stalk, and frequently lies prone on the ground with the small flowers more or less injured with dust and sand. This variety also blooms until late in October. Toad-flax is first cousin to the beautiful garden snapdragon (*Antirrhinum majus*), which is resplendent in purple, violet-blue, and transparent white. *A. maurandioides* is a Texan and Mexican variety in cultivation with violet flowers which spring from the leaf axils. *A. Orontium* is a pale purplish flower, and a weed of old gardens; the plant is smaller than the preceding one.

JULY TO OCTOBER. 175

Common Yarrow.
Achillea Millefolium.

Yarrow is the commonest kind of a common weed, whose gray-white flower heads are utterly unattractive even to those who profess to be fond of flowers. But, before passing the weed in disdain, it will be worth our while to pick a small piece and place it under the glass for closer inspection. Ah! what a change! —the uninteresting weed at once assumes an attractive look. The little gray centers, which are called the flower heads, are minutely and perfectly formed, and are as symmetrically arranged as the markings on what we call "brain coral." Around these flower heads are four, sometimes five, white rays. There is a pretty pink variety of the yarrow, in which these rays instead of being

Yarrow.

white are delicately tinted with pink. I found this variety quite plentiful in an old cemetery in Campton, N. H. The yarrow blooms from July until October. It has a pleasant herby smell.

Indian Tobacco. The Indian tobacco (from which is
Lobelia inflata. obtained a noted quack medicine) is one of the least interesting of our blue wild flowers; it is quite common in some of the poorest fields of New York and Massachusetts. I never happened to meet the plant in New Hampshire—one does not always find everything in one spot, and as the search was confined to a limited region in the latter State, I have no doubt that several varieties of *Lobelia* might be found there—but there is plenty of Indian tobacco in the vicinity of Boston. This variety grows about one foot high and bears on the tip of the stem a number of purple flowers which resemble the cultivated variety called *L. erinus*, which comes to us from the Cape of Good Hope. On the banks of the Pemigewasset River, in shady places where the ground is wet, will be found the smaller *L. Kalmii;* this variety bears pretty little blue-purple flowers—much prettier and bluer than Indian tobacco. *L. syphilitica* is the largest variety of this flower, but, in my estimation, not the prettiest. Its flowers are pale and purplish; and, although they are arranged showily on a stalk about twenty inches high, they can not be called

handsome, like their relative the cardinal flower. It is perfectly plain in this instance that *color* is the most important element of beauty in a flower. The *Lobelias* bloom in midsummer.

Cardinal Flower. The magnificent red of the cardinal
Lobelia cardinalis. flower fully entitles it to its name. There is no other wild flower which approaches it in color. In August the flower is in its prime, and it will be found in marshy ground and on the edge of the pasture, where the partial shade of the neighboring woods relieves the bright red in a very charming fashion. I have found the flower in the Catskills, but never in the White Mountains; it is common in the Berkshires, and grows here and there over the country in a latitude, generally speaking, not north of

Cardinal Flower.

Albany. But, again, I must claim that this is a limitation based only upon personal experience. At any rate, I do not consider the flower common, as I have searched for it in vain in many of the moist meadows of New Hampshire. The brilliant blossom is peculiarly formed; it has two narrow lateral flanges, and beneath these droop the three broader points of the lower lip; above this the corolla tube sticks straight out with a touch of yellow at its tip. This tube is so narrow and long that the bees have no luck in the hunt for honey; it is very amusing to see how bothered they are about getting in—of course they have to give it up! Then a humming bird comes along, balancing himself before the slender tube, and easily licks all the honey out with his long tongue.

The beautiful, brilliant flower is so often seen beside a pool of water that Dr. Holmes's verse exactly describes its environment:

> " The cardinal, and the blood-red spots,
>   Its double in the stream;
> As if some wounded eagle's breast,
>   Slow throbbing o'er the plain,
> Had left its airy path impressed
>   In drops of scarlet rain."

Wild Sunflower. By the middle of summer the wild
Helianthus giganteus. sunflower appears here and there beside the road, with its light-yellow disks lighting up the shadows which are cast by the neighboring

trees and brightening for a season the dense leafy growth which fills the nooks and corners of the wayside. The plant grows about four feet high,

Wild Sunflower.

and has rather narrow, dark-green leaves which have a rough feeling. The flower is at the most only three inches in diameter; its center is a deeper yellow than the rays, and often a trifle greenish. My impression of the general appearance of this wild sunflower is that it is prolific in green leaves and sparing in yellow flowers, in this respect showing a great contrast with its cultivated garden relative (a flower of the same size) called Sutton's Miniature. This last-named variety is as abundant in golden bloom as it is in shiny, birchlike leafage. But, between the two varieties, perhaps the wild sunflower is more dainty and delicate in both color and form; its fault is rather that we do not see enough of it.

Tansy. Tansy is the
Tanacetum vulgare. very common
yellow flower which looks like a thick cluster of ox-eye daisies with the white rays all picked off. The name comes from its character of durability; it is a corruption of *Athanasia*, meaning undying. It blooms and smells strong all summer, and, dried, lasts and smells stronger all winter. The plant is gathered by the country folk, who dry it in the kitchen and make a perfectly vile tasting tea of its leaves, which is said

Tansy.

to be excellent in assisting measles "to come out" on the children who are suffering with it in an incipient stage. Alas for the children!—the cure is nearly as bad as the disease. Tansy grows everywhere, and one can easily find it by the road or in the field. It came here from Europe. I never found any in the Pemigewasset Valley, but it is common in every village in Massachusetts; it is also plentiful in the region of the Catskill Mountains. Its aromatic smell is far from unpleasant.

Wild Carrot.
Daucus Carota.
The wild carrot, sometimes called bird's nest, is a familiar flower of every wayside and pasture. Its head of grayish green-white flowers is broad and concave at the top, and before it has quite reached maturity it is hollowed exactly like a bird's nest; so the flower is appropriately named. Under the magnifying glass the tiny flowers at once lose all appearance of confusion, and reveal a regularity of growth quite unexpected by the casual observer; the little petals are

Wild Carrot.

more or less unequal, but not enough so to make the flowers look deformed; on the margin of the cluster they are large and more perfect. There is a certain intricacy in the details of the plant which makes one think it looks fussy; but this idea is relinquished as soon as it is examined under the glass, and we are impressed with the fact that Nature's handiwork, when it comes to little things, is simply exquisite. The wild carrot was brought to this country from Europe, and is common in New York State and in many localities down East; but I have found very few specimens in New Hampshire. It flowers in midsummer, and its general resemblance to caraway at once points to the fact that the two plants are closely related.

Mullein.
Verbascum Thapsus. The mullein, whose rugged perpendicular stalk is seen rising from its stony setting in a hillside pasture, is a familiar object with every one, North and South. Here, again, is another native of the Old World. It is a strange circumstance that many of our most familiar summer wild flowers are *not*

Mullein.

American, while those that *are* do not, as a rule, frequent the roadsides or the waste places around our cities. The steeple bush and the cardinal flower, for instance, prefer the open country; but tansy, chicory, wild carrot, thorn-apple, and toadflax are veritable tramps who keep company with each other on the outskirts of every town and city. But the mullein prefers the pasture land, where, on the edge of some hillock, it often poses for the artist in a picturesque costume of pale yellow and green, with its feet hidden among the gray stones, and its head relieved by the somber background of a gray thundercloud. Nothing is softer or more delicate in color than the pale-green, velvety leaves when they first appear above ground. The flowers bloom all summer.

Chicory.
Cichorium Intybus.

Chicory is one of our prettiest blue flowers; it is blue enough to call it blue, although I must call attention to the fact that blue in a pure state does not exist on the petal of *any* flower, wild or cultivated. I might with justice except the familiar forget-me-not, whose quality of color is very nearly a pure one. But chicory sometimes shows a very good blue, so we will not quarrel with it. The little flower straps are singularly like those of the dandelion, and this fact betrays its close relationship with the latter flower. Not only these straps, but the center of the flower (the stamens and styles) looks very much like the dandelion. Under the microscope the chicory blossom shows a charming misty purple-blue color which one wishes might be oftener seen among our wild flowers. It is common in western New York and in many parts of New Jersey; but Gray says it is "mainly east," meaning east, possibly, of such a point as Buffalo. However, in many localities north and northeast of Boston it is quite absent. It can be found in almost any empty lot in either Brooklyn or Philadelphia, but I have never seen it in the hill country south of the White Mountains, or in the vicinity of Lake Champlain. It blooms from June to October. Endive (*C. Endivia*), the slightly bitter root leaves of which make an excellent salad, is a very near relative of the blue chicory.

Chicory.

JULY TO OCTOBER. 185

Common Everlasting.
Gnaphalium polycephalum.

Everlasting is so well known by every one that it needs no description here; yet the little white flowers are so much like miniature pond lilies under the microscope that the resemblance is amusing, and the regularly formed little thing becomes beautiful; but what appears to be tiny white petals are in reality a number of scales called the involucre, or flower envelop; the central whitish or yellow part constitutes the flower head. An analysis of this under a rather powerful glass is quite interesting. The plant is conspicuous in every field by its cottony foliage, which is pale sage-green in color. Pearly everlasting (*Anaphalis margaritacea*) has a broader flower cluster, is generally whiter, and grows in dry fields and near the woods.

Everlasting.

Bur-Marigold, or Beggar-ticks.
Bidens frondosa.

The bur-marigold is a wretched weed with rather pretty conventional leafage, but unattractive rusty-yellow flowers without rays. The seed vessels are barb-pointed and catch on one's clothes and in the wool of sheep, and are thus transported to different localities. I remember spending "oceans" of time divesting my woolen stockings of the thorny little objects, which I had gathered unawares in the passage through a pasture on a certain slope of the White Hills. A knickerbocker suit is undoubtedly best adapted to mountain tramps, but one is a "tramp" in reality if his stockings encounter the magic touch of the beggar-ticks. Each separate seed vessel demands individual attention; brushes are of no avail. The bur-marigold blooms in August.

Bidens chrysanthemoides.

There is another variety, called *B. chrysanthemoides*, which bears pretty yellow-rayed flowers about two inches in diameter which resemble coreopsis; the bur-marigold, in fact, is closely related to the coreopsis and sunflower, and the general resemblance of all three may be accounted for as a family likeness. *B. chrysanthemoides* grows in wet places and reaches a height of about two feet.

Bouncing Bet, or Soapwort. *Saponaria officinalis.*

Bouncing Bet comes to us from Europe; she is a cultivated rather than a wild character. Still, she has escaped the confines of the garden, and may be found any day in summer basking in the sunshine beside the road and in the vicinity of some old homestead. The flowers are the most delicate crimson pink imaginable—a tint so light that we might call it a pinkish white. It is well to notice that the joints of the plant have a swollen appearance; this is a characteristic feature of members of the Pink family, to which the soapwort belongs. The plant grows from one to two feet high.

Bouncing Bet.

CHAPTER XIII.

JULY, AUGUST, AND SEPTEMBER.
Petunia to Tritoma.

Petunia.
P. nyctaginiflora and P. violacea.

THE garden annual petunia gets its name from *petun*, the aboriginal term for tobacco. It belongs to the Nightshade family, and is a near relative of common tobacco. The species *P. nyctaginiflora* and *P. violacea* and their hybrids are the common petunias of our gardens. The former variety is white, and may still be obtained from the seedsmen under that name. The latter variety, with originally purple and magenta flowers, has now become so changed by supercultivation that it is rarely presented in its primitive form. The finest of all the petunias are called Giants of California; they are hybrids raised in that country by a lady

Giant of California, Petunia.

whose health demanded outdoor exercise in a warm, sunny climate;* these flowers measure four or five inches across and possess exceedingly delicate and brilliant hues. Another beautiful petunia is called Green Margin. It is supposed that a green flower does not exist; but I have raised in my garden specimens of this variety showing a broad corolla eighty per cent of which was bright green; the rest was magenta veined with ultramarine. Molucca Balm is another green flower sometimes seen in old gardens. The petunia is strong in purple-reds and steel-blues, colors which are not sufficiently appreciated for their sober beauty. There are several paintings by that most spiritual artist, Edward Burne-Jones, in which it is evident he has imitated the petunia's colors. I might instance the one entitled "The Baleful Head," where the armor of Perseus is exactly the steel-blue-purple color of the outside of a magenta petunia. *Kermesina splendens* is a lovely variety with flowers of a rich crimson-

Molucca Balm.

---

* This magnificent strain of petunias was discovered among Mr. W. Atlee Burpie's Defiance petunias (another strain of splendid color and form) by Mrs. T. Gould, of Ventura, Cal. The Giants of California, which I have cultivated with great success, were raised from seed obtained from Peter Henderson & Co., New York. The varieties were named Aurora, Midnight, Titania, and Rainbow.

magenta hue. The double varieties I do not consider æsthetically a success. The plants bloom through summer and early autumn. Two near relatives of the petunia are *Nicotiana affinis*, a sweet-scented, white-flowered tobacco, whose blossoms open toward evening, and *N. Tabacum*, with funnel-formed, pink-edged flowers which have no perfume; the latter variety is hardly beautiful enough to deserve a place in the garden, and I have banished it from mine. The tobacco blooms in late summer and early autumn.

Nicotiana Affinis.

Larkspur.
Delphinium.

The larkspur of our gardens comes variously from Europe, Siberia, and China. It has a lovely spear of deep blue or purple flowers which gracefully waves to and fro in every passing zephyr. It flowers in summer. *D. formosum cœlestinum* is a charming large-flowered variety with a soft, light, ultramarine-blue color. *D. elatum* (Bee Larkspur) is cultivated from Europe, and is quite tall, bearing flowers in a great variety of colors, both single and double. These varieties are perennial. *D. Consolida* is a European annual variety which has here and there escaped from the garden to the roadside. *D. Ajacis* (Rocket Larkspur) is a common garden variety like the foregoing, except that the flowers are crowded in a long raceme (stalk), and are more showy; and the spur is shorter. It has something like ten distinct varieties of color, mostly ranging through blue, purple, and crimson. There are three varieties native to this country, which are found mostly south and west of Pennsylvania. They are named *D. azureum*, with blue or white flowers which appear in spring; *D. tricorne*, a dwarf variety one foot high with flowers like the foregoing, but more showy; and *D. exaltatum*, a tall variety resembling the garden rocket, which flowers in summer. These wild varieties are all perennials. A very beautiful blue variety, which grows wild among the Pyrenees, is called *D. peregrinum;* this is one of the bluest wild flowers I have ever seen, excepting the gentians of the Alps and Pyrenees. Larkspur is a member of the Crowfoot family, and is therefore related to the buttercup, nigella, columbine, monkshood, baneberry, and black snakeroot.

Larkspur.

Hollyhock.
Althæa rosea.

The old-fashioned hollyhock still holds its place in the modern garden, but the old single variety is rapidly being displaced by a new double one which is as full as the fullest rose and quite as beautiful. The colors of these double flowers are rose-pink, salmon, white, primrose-yellow, lilac, magenta, deep red, and maroon. Unfortunately, the double variety is not as hardy as the single, but it is more beautiful in point of color effect. For form I still consider the single flower unsurpassed in beauty, and most decorative. The hollyhock comes to us from Syria. It flowers in summer and early autumn. The marsh mallow (*A. officinalis*), the root of which is used to make marsh mallow paste, is a very near relative of the hollyhock, and grows wild on our Eastern coast. The clusters of flowers are pale crimson-pink; the corolla is about an inch in diameter. Musk mallow (*Malva moschata*), formerly common in old-fashioned gardens but now frequently met with beside the road, is also a relative of the hollyhock; one has only to look the little flower square in the face to recognize at once a family likeness between it and the queenly garden favorite. The flowers of musk mallow are white, or extremely pale magenta-pink; the leaves are cut into slender lobes. It blooms in summer. *M. rotundifolia* is a little plant with heart-shaped leaves and pink-white flowers, which is found in similar situations.

Scarlet Rose-Mallow.
Hibiscus coccineus.

Prof. Meehan calls the scarlet rose-mallow "probably the most gorgeous of all the plants indigenous to the United States," and I think he is quite right. A glorious red-scarlet flower it certainly is, and scarlet wild flowers are extremely rare—in fact, it would be difficult for me to think of more than this one. The cardinal flower is not scarlet, but intense red. This scarlet mallow grows in deep marshes near the coast from Carolina southward. It has been cultivated and grows well in the North, if it is placed in the greenhouse during the cold months. The flower has five large petals, and measures six or eight inches across. *H. Moscheutos* (Swamp Rose-Mallow) is a similar flower with pale-pink petals, which grows in the North. Both bloom in late summer. *H.*

Scarlet Rose-Mallow.

Syriacus is the name of the shrubby althæa, or rose of sharon, which has a flower like the single hollyhock, and thus unmistakably shows its relationship with the latter flower. It is a native of the Levant, and flowers in late summer and early autumn. It is interesting to know that cotton (*Gossypium herbaceum*) is a member of the Mallow family, and is therefore a distant relative of the hollyhock.

Blazing-Star.
Liatris scariosa.

The blazing-star is a beautiful common wild flower, whose spherical, purple flower-clusters are thickly or thinly, as the case may be, arranged along the tall stem which in New England, in swampy places by the sea, attains a height of four or five feet. Out West the plant does not grow so high, but it is very common, according to accounts of Prof. Meehan, in Indian Territory, and is found as far south as Florida. The purple flowers are very beautiful, and remind one of the garden beauty called mourning bride (*Scabiosa*). The plant is in bloom in late summer.

Blazing-Star.

Viper's Bugloss, or Blueweed.
Echium vulgare.

Along the banks of the Hudson, beside Esopus Creek, and on waste ground, in parts of the country where civilization has its strongest foothold, there the blueweed's seeds have obtained a lodgment; but I have not found it yet in the fields of New Hampshire. Gray says it came to us from the old gardens of Europe, and has become a weed in the fields from Pennsylvania to Virginia and southward, but I have found it on the banks of the Neponset River near Boston, and it is very common in the vicinity of Hoboken. It possesses a charming æsthetic color; the green is soft and silvery, and the blossom is violet-blue when open and crimson-pink when in the bud. The curving lines of the flower-bearing branches are very beautiful. The plant is rough and bristly, grows about two feet high, and blooms during the early summer and on into September. *Lycopsis arvensis* (small bugloss), about a foot high, bears smaller blue flowers on a bristly stem. It is rarer than blueweed.

Viper's Bugloss, or Blueweed.

Monkshood.
Aconitum uncinatum.

Aconite, or monkshood is a native of Virginia, but it finds its way northward along the Alleghanies until it reaches New Jersey; and, although it is not common in the latter State, it can be found here and there beside some little stream, hanging its dark-purple hoods over the grass and neighboring weeds. Its slender stems and loose hanging flowers remind one of the columbine, but its manner of growth is almost vinelike; it appears as though it would climb. The top of the flower looks like a helmet. It blooms in summer and in September.

Gladiolus.
Gladiolus communis, and psittacinus.

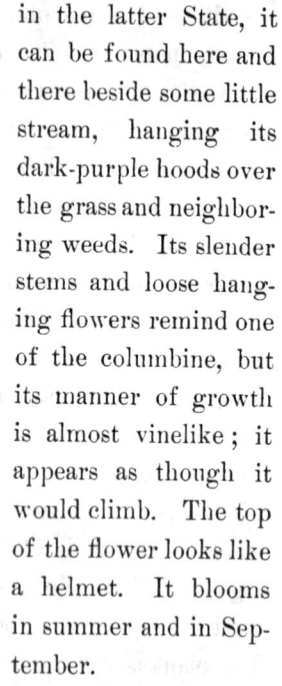

The gladiolus is still a great favorite of the garden, but it has been so much improved by hybridiza-

Monkshood.

tion that the old red and pink varieties are supplanted by an infinite number of brilliant-hued flowers, many of which come from M. Lemoine, the eminent horticulturist of France. *G. communis* comes from Europe, and bears pink and pink-striped white flowers; *G. Byzantinus*, of the Levant, bears larger and more brilliantly colored flowers; *G. blandus* is the parent of some of the white and pale-colored flowers; *G. cardinalis* is the parent of the intense red variety, some of whose flowers have a white stripe on each of the three lower divisions. These are quite common. *G. psittacinus* is a tall species with large yellow flowers somewhat striped with reddish color; this and *G. cardinalis* are the parents of G. Gandavensis (commonly cultivated), from which so many subvarieties have been produced. But the fact is, these three last varieties (excepting G. Gandavensis) it would be difficult for an inexperienced person to identify among so great a host of hybrids. They come from the Cape of Good Hope. The flowers named in the seedsmen's catalogues are more easily found in the garden. Brenchleyensis is a common, intense red flower; Lemoine's Butterfly is beautifully streaked and blotched in a variety of colors; Chrysolora is one of the finest yellow varieties; Madame Monneret is a beautiful rose-pink variety, and Ceres is a combination of white and magenta-pink. There are an infinite number of other beautifully colored flowers, but these varieties I mention are "personally known" to me and are like old friends. I can testify to their beauty. The gladiolus blooms in late summer and early autumn.

Tiger Flower. The charming *Tigridia*, or tiger flower, which looks like a scarlet or yellow iris, comes to us from Mexico. It flowers in summer and continues sometimes into September. It is a pity the blossoms are so frail; they rarely last after midday. The center of the flower is spotted like an orchid.

Tigridia Pavonia.

Tiger Flower.

Mexican Star Flower. The sweet-scented little Mexican star flower is becoming popular in the garden; as its name indicates, it usually blooms, two flowers at a time; the flower stalk is Y-shaped with a starlike, white blossom on each branch. There are a couple of long, slender leaves that look like grass; indeed, the whole plant is so simple and modest that it can not fail to please those who have the most fastidious taste. Another Mexican flower, *Bessera elegans* (or coral drops), is a

Milla biflora.

frequent companion of the *Milla biflora*, and has graceful little clusters of pumpkin-orange flowers striped with cream-color; the leaves are also grass-like. Both flowers bloom in summer. The *Cyclobothra flava* is a pretty little russet-yellow flower which I grow with the foregoing in one of the large tubs of my garden, where these dainty characters will show to the best advantage. Its slim stems remind one slightly of carnation stalks; the flowers are shaped like tiny inverted tulips. It is a native of California, and belongs to the Lily family.

Spanish Bayonet.
Yucca filamentosa and aloifolia.

The yuccas (*filamentosa* and *aloifolia*) are Southern plants, extending into Mexico, and are cultivated for ornament; they are not quite hardy in the extreme North, but in New York and southward they stand the winter cold well. *Y. angustifolia* and *gloriosa* are less frequently met with. The flowers are all a beautiful cream-white color; sometimes they are tinged with purple. They bloom in summer.

Tritoma.
Tritoma Uvaria.

Tritoma is an old-fashioned favorite which goes by the popular name of red-hot-poker, and warms up the garden by blooming in late summer. It comes from the Cape of Good Hope. The flowers are most peculiarly graded through yellow into dull scarlet, without seeming to touch orange; they look like exaggerated grape-hyacinths (*Muscari botryoides*) in reddish color instead of blue. But the two flowers are related—they belong to the Lily family. The grape-hyacinth has escaped from the garden to the field; it bears a dense cluster of tiny blue-violet flowers in early spring. Our common hyacinth (*H. orientalis*), which comes from the Levant, is likewise a family connection. It is too well known to need any description here. The hyacinth presents yellow, red, and blue under modified conditions; it is characteristic of spring, but is more of a hothouse than a garden flower. It seems a pity that the hyacinth and the crocus, the latter a flower of easy cultivation and resplendent in color, should be less popular in the garden than the showy Lady Washington geraniums (Pelargoniums) of the summer season; but such seems to be the case. The Lady Washington geraniums, I might add (the name is applied without much restriction to the flowering geraniums), are really those varieties with shrubby stems known as P. cucullatum (cowled P.), P. cordatum (heart-leaved P.), and P. angulosum (maple-leaved P.), whose flowers sometimes measure two inches across.

CHAPTER XIV.

JULY, AUGUST, AND SEPTEMBER.
Coreopsis to Ladies' Tresses.

Coreopsis. BRIGHT-EYED coreopsis is one of the
Coreopsis tinctoria. cheeriest of our smaller garden flowers, and it is another distinctly American character. The variety *C. tinctoria*, of Arkansas, is the common coreopsis, or calliopsis of all country gardens. It has extremely narrow leaflets, a smooth, waving, and somewhat wiry stem, and numerous flowers, which are small and beautifully variegated with wine-red and golden yellow; one variety has tubular rays, but it lacks effect. *C. Drummondii* is a beautiful large golden-yellow flower with a dark-red spot on each ray, and leaves composed of oval-shaped leaflets; *C. coronata* is a flower with broad and hand-

Coreopsis.

some golden-yellow rays whose red spot is very small, and a disk which is yellow instead of brown. The leaves are oblong, with three to five divisions. Both of these varieties come from Texas, and they produce larger and finer flowers in the cultivated state. All three of the varieties mentioned are annuals; there are two perennial varieties which are not quite so common in the garden—they are *C. lanceolata* and *C. auriculata*. Both grow wild in the West and South, and both have entirely yellow flowers. The former variety is commonly cultivated by the florists; the latter is taller and is leafy almost to the top; both flower in early summer. The coreopsis is a very near relative of the bur-marigold, and it closely resembles the variety of that flower named *Bidens chrysanthemoides*. In the garden, coreopsis blooms all summer and as late as September.

Dahlia.
Dahlia variabilis.

The common garden dahlia is also a near relative of coreopsis. It comes to us from Mexico. I fear we do not sufficiently appreciate the fact that we are indebted to this country and not to Europe for a great many of our most beautiful garden flowers. The tuberose, Poinsettia (*Euphorbia pulcherrima*), *Tigridia*, *Milla biflora*, *Bessera elegans*, zinnia, marigold, and *yucca* all come from Mexico. The dahlia is named for a Swedish botanist, Dahl, a contemporary of the great botanist

Linnæus. Its large, conventional double flowers are, in my estimation, not quite as beautiful as the single ones. It blooms throughout the summer and in September.

Marigold.
Tagetes patula, and erecta.

The marigold is an old garden favorite which has of late years been greatly improved by the efforts of the horticulturists. The common single varieties of years ago no longer have a place in our gardens. There are three distinct varieties: the African, *T. erecta*, the French *T. patula*, and *T. signata*. These are again subdivided, on account of their distinct types, as follows:

T. erecta.	African El Dorado, an immense flower which sometimes reaches a diameter of four inches.
	African quilled, smaller, with quilled rays.
	African dwarf double, smaller plants.
T. patula.	French tall, reaching a height of two feet.
	French dwarf, not over a foot high.
	Both varieties double.
T. signata.	French (Legion d'Honneur), small single yellow flowers with claret-spotted rays; height not over seven inches.

These types are quite distinct and are therefore readily recognized. The names African and French are misleading; the plants originally came from South America and Mexico. They are prolific bloomers, and continue in flower from June until the middle of October, when they are pretty sure of a veto on further production by Jack Frost! I have had a symmetrical plant in my garden, of the French order, which bore at one time seventy-five blossoms in various stages of development. The dark pinnate foliage, decorative in character, and the rich yellow-orange flowers, gave the plant a distinguished appearance very far removed from the commonplace. There was a touch of conventionality about it which was quaint and old-fashioned as well as refreshing in the midst of surroundings altogether modern; asters of the most approved type, poppies of rousing proportions and rarest colors, sweet peas of the newest varieties, mourning brides in the latest fashion of black, and a host of new annuals which the old-fashioned garden never saw. But the marigold of the French order has still an atmosphere of old times about it, particularly if we happen to catch the odor

El Dorado Marigold.

Legion d'Honneur Marigold.

of a freshly plucked flower. How quickly the familiar strong scent carries us back in imagination to our grandmothers' gardens! The seed of the marigold germinates in a remarkably short space of time. If it is soaked awhile in very warm water, and then planted an eighth of an inch deep in light soil, in some position where it gets the full benefit of the warm sunshine, the baby plant will push its way to the air above in thirty-six hours; ten weeks should then elapse before the plant begins to bloom; the few flowers which may appear before this time are premature and poorly developed. Young plants forced into early bloom by a beginning in the greenhouse ultimately amount to little.

The colors of the marigold are extraordinary: golden yellow, orange-yellow, pure lemon-yellow, russet-red edged with gold, and golden yellow spotted with brownish-claret color—these are all rendered in the purest tones on the gracefully curled rays.

Zinnia.
Zinnia elegans.

The garden zinnia has only one palpable fault: it is unmistakably stiff. Yet, putting aside this little defect, we may certainly consider it a gifted flower. It has an astonishing range of color, which comprehends nearly the whole scale—white, cream, buff, pale yellow, deep yellow, lemon-yellow somewhat toned down, orange, light orange, scarlet, crimson, magenta, the three pink tints which are dilutions of these three reds, perfectly pure pink, lilac, dull purple, dull violet, maroon, and, finest of all, an intense deep red generally called Jacqueminot-color.* This last I consider a glorious flower whose full beauty can only be seen under a bright artificial light. The zinnia, like the marigold, comes from Mexico, and it blooms all summer and throughout September. Besides the colors I have mentioned there are a great number of æsthetic ones of that delightfully subdued quality which we call crushed strawberry, heliotrope, and so forth. The flower grows nearly as large as the largest marigold, and is somewhat of the same shape; in one variety the rays are curled and twisted,† but in all the others they have a uniform reflex curve; it is an annual, and grows readily in common garden soil.

Mourning Bride. The mourning bride (*Scabiosa atro-*
Scabiosa *purpurea*) has of late been greatly
atropurpurea. improved; it was a favorite of the old-fashioned garden, but the newer varieties are so much larger and finer than the old that it would scarcely be recognized as the same flower. The colors are also greatly improved; they are white, pale

---

* This variety I have obtained from Peter Henderson & Co., New York.

† Curled and crested zinnia. This remarkable variety was brought out a few years ago by Peter Henderson & Co., New York.

rose, deep pink, purple, palest yellow, and rich, dark claret-maroon color. The last-mentioned variety is most beautiful; it has the effect of a fine piece of beadwork; the tiny anthers are pale lilac; and the corollas, funnel-formed, are the richest, darkest wine-red color imaginable; the whole effect of the flower is *black*, and it is well named Black Scabiosa. The flower stem is exceedingly long and stiff, as well as bare. The leafage is variously shaped, but in general slightly resembles that of the common wild daisy, except that it is larger and broader. It blooms in late summer. The flower might deceive one as to its family connection; it looks like a Composite, but Gray has given it the position of the latter's next-door neighbor. It belongs to the Teasel family. The distinguishing differences which separate it from its Composite neighbors are four *separate* stamens to each corolla (Composites have their five stamens tied together by the connecting anthers, which form a tube inclosing the style) and an ovary, which becomes an akene in fruit containing a *hanging* seed. The seeds of the Composites do not hang, but are borne in stout shell-like akenes.

Mourning bride comes to us from the Old World. Sometimes it is called the pincushion-flower; the light-colored anthers certainly *do* suggest pinheads. Wild teasel (*Dipsacus sylvestris*) is a weed I have occasionally found along the roadsides in New Hampshire, and it is closely related to the *Scabiosa*. It has rather prickly stems, uninteresting lilac flower heads, somewhat reminding one of *Scabiosa*, except that they are oblong, and leaves which are united round the stem. This is the nearest approach to *Scabiosa* among the wild flowers of this country.

Sunflower. The sunflower is distinctly American,
Helianthus annuus. and comprises a large, varied, and interesting division of the Composite family. *H. annuus* is the large-flowered variety common in our gardens; but there are many new varieties, some smaller and some double, which are more beautiful. A favorite small flower, about the size of *Rudbekia* and similar to it in appearance, is called Sutton's Miniature. A splendid large, double flower, resembling a big yellow chrysanthemum, is named Globosus fistulosus; its color is a magnificent golden-yellow, and its figure is very decorative. Oscar Wilde is an extremely tall variety, with small single flowers, which bloom in great profusion. *H. argophyllus* is a native of Texas, and is cultivated for the sake of its beautiful white foliage; its flowers are large and sin-

gle. Primrose is a lovely light-yellow flower with a dark center; the flowers are borne along the tall stem from within a couple of feet of the ground. Of the wild species the commonest is *H. giganteus*. In the pine district of New Jersey and southward is another common variety with long, narrow leaves and small flowers with dark centers, named *H. angustifolius*. *H. occidentalis* is a Western variety with flowers whose disks as well as rays are yellow, and leaves which are broad below, but quite narrow above, on a stalk not over three feet high. *H. heterophyllus* is a Southern variety, which has flowers with dark purple-brown disks and golden rays, and leaves oval and lance-shaped. The flowers are very few and are borne on long stems. Maximilian's Sunflower is a Western variety under cultivation, whose small flower has a yellow disk. *H. annuus* and *H. argophyllus* are annuals; all the other wild varieties are perennials. The sunflower blooms in late summer and in September.

Snow on the Mountain.
Euphorbia marginata.

Snow on the mountain, which is a beautiful plant growing wild east and west of the Mississippi, is rapidly coming in favor as a garden ornament. It grows about two feet high, and its oval leaves are broadly white-margined; those at the top of the plant are nearly if not altogether white; it is an annual which flowers in late summer. The flower itself is inconspicuous, but the five white petal-like appendages and the white leafage are the interesting part of the plant; *Euphorbia pulcherrima*, or Poinsettia, is its near relative, which comes to us from Mexico. This variety is characterized by a group of bright scarlet leaves terminating the branches. It is most successful as a hothouse plant in the colder climate of the North, and its insignificant flowers, surrounded by the vermilion leaves, appear in the winter. The plant was named for Mr. Poinsett, who was minister to Mexico in 1828 and also secretary of war under President Van Buren.

Maximilian's Sunflower.

Fireweed.
Great Willow-herb.
Epilobium angustifolium.

The fireweed, curiously enough, flourishes on ground which has been at some time burned over. That tract of country which lies between Montpelier and Wells

River, Vt., is rugged and covered with a wild and tangled forest which has been subjected to the woodman's axe. This means (as every one knows who is familiar with the lumber companies and their dealings with New England forests) a devastation of the land by fire as well as axe. Consequently this particular tract of land I have alluded to is peculiarly rich in fine specimens of the magenta-pink fireweed. Beautiful tall spires of the delicate flower are seen everywhere in the blackened clearings—I say clearings, because they are called such, but in point of fact the fireweed decorates and cheers a wretched-looking waste which would more appropriately go by the name of chaos. I know of another spot, in the Pemi-

Fireweed.

gewasset Valley, where a sawmill was burned several years ago, and now the site is covered by a luxuriantly shrubby growth of fireweed, which in August is a glory of magenta-pink color. One may easily understand why it is called Willow-herb, as its leaf is exactly like that of the swamp willow. In September the pretty heads of magenta flowers are transformed into clusters of curved and twisted seed-vessels which are constantly shedding a disheveled mass of stringy white silk, reminding one, perhaps, of the wild gray hair of witches caught in the thicket.

It seems scarcely necessary to call attention to the fact that the fireweed is closely related to the evening primrose: a comparison of the two flowers shows a remarkable similarity between them.

Joe-Pye Weed.
Eupatorium purpureum.

Joe-Pye weed, oddly named for a New England Indian doctor, is rather a conspicuous dull pale-magenta flower whose fuzzy head towers five or six feet above the lowlands in late summer and early autumn. The plant will always be associated in my mind with Indian doctors, who, by the way, have not yet finished their "herb cures" among the country folk. There is such a doctor in a New England village but four miles from my summer home, who, I am given to understand, does a thriving business—or shall I say commands a wide practice?—in a certain locality of cultured New England! But we will not insinuate anything regarding New England culture in connection

Joe-Pye Weed.

with quacks; so we will pass on from Joe-Pye weed and Indian doctors to boneset.

Boneset.
Eupatorium perfoliatum.
This is a very close relative of the other plant, and is also a favorite herb among the country folk, for whom it furnishes a popular medicine. Who does not know all about "boneset tea," and who likes it?

But boneset taffy (taken for a cough) was quite another thing, and children used to be very tolerant of it for reasons which it is unnecessary to explain. The plant grows about three feet high, has a spreading leaf (more correctly a pair of leaves) through the middle of which the main stem appears to pass, and bears a head of small, fuzzy white flowers which are not bright or attractive enough to look pretty. The plant flowers in late summer and frequents low meadows.

Ladies' Tresses. Toward the end of
Spiranthes cernua. summer and through September the sweet smelling tiny flowers called ladies' tresses may be found in the swamps or in the wet meadows. The little plant is easily identified by the spiral growth of the white blossoms about the stem, which is not often over eight inches tall. This flower belongs to the Orchis family, and is a near relative of the pink and yellow moccason-flowers which bloom in the spring and early summer. There is another variety of ladies' tresses, called *S. gracilis*, which grows in dry ground

S. Cernua.

or on the side of a hill; this has a slenderer spike with fewer flowers, which are often less twisted than those of the other variety. The rattlesnake plantain is closely related to ladies' tresses—a fact which is not surprising, as the appearance of the two flower spikes is somewhat similar.

CHAPTER XV.

AUGUST TO NOVEMBER.

Golden-rod and Asters.

Golden-rod.
Solidago.

THE name golden-rod conjures up the thought of an immense family of flowers thirty odd members of which a person with a fair knowledge of botany may easily identify without searching through a wide tract of country, and possibly without wandering but a few yards beyond the highways of our Northeastern States. In a quarter-mile length of a road in Campton, N. H., I have

S. Arguta. found no less than fifteen varieties of the flower, "all well defined" (to quote the words of Coleridge in reference to the smells of Cologne). But this is rather unusual, and a short exploration of a field, hillside, shady glen, and unfrequented wayside might result in as good if not a better "find." There are a few very common varieties of the golden-rod which may be recognized at once by the following characteristics:

S. arguta is perhaps the earliest golden-rod, and will be found sometimes in full bloom in the middle of July. Its sharply toothed leaf is feather-veined—that is, the veins spring outward from each side of the middle rib, just as the smaller divisions of a feather spring from its quill. The main stem is smooth. The slender flower stems, bearing greenish-yellow (in effect) flowers, spread widely apart and droop.

S. altissima, one of the lowest of the common varieties, is never over four feet high and resembles *S. arguta*, but it has a rough, hairy stem and a very veiny leaf which is broad-lance-shaped and toothed. It has one-sided, curved flower clusters which are bright yellow.

S. ulmifolia (elm-leaved golden-rod) is a similar variety. Gray says,

S. Ulmifolia.

"Too near *S. altissima*—distinguished only by its smooth stem and thin, larger leaves." Both these varieties are early-flowering.

S. nemoralis is not over two feet high, and has dense plumes of rich golden-yellow flowers growing on the upper side of their stems; the main stem is grayish, with a cottony look, and is sparingly furnished with dull gray-green leaves. It blooms in early August, and is found mostly in sterile fields. I consider it the most brilliantly colored of all the golden-rods.

S. Canadensis is coarse-growing, has rough, hairy stems and leaves which are harsh to the touch; the thick clusters of deep-yellow flowers grow in a one-sided way on their spreading stems; the leaves are distinctly three-veined (more correctly speaking, three-ribbed). This variety will grow from three to five feet high, or may be higher.

S. Nemoralis.

S. rugosa is sometimes distinguished by a number of smaller branches with little leaves, terminating with small flower clusters loosely grouped. The stocky stem has broad leaves, and grows nearly as tall as *S. Canadensis.* It is an early-flowering species.

S. lanceolata is a variety whose tall stem is set with narrow leaves without teeth, and is terminated with a dense flat-topped flower cluster, which is greenish yellow in color effect. The plume of this variety is too flat and bunchy to be confused with the gracefully curved ones of the other varieties.

S. tenuifolia is a variety similar to *S. lanceolata* but with slenderer leaves and narrower or more club-shaped little flowers. The leaves are one-nerved and rather crowded on the stem; the flower clusters are smaller than those of *S. lanceolata.* It grows in sandy ground, and near the coast.

S. Canadensis.

Three-ribbed Leaf.

S. Rugosa.

S. sempervirens is a tall seashore variety common in salt marshes and among the rocks. It may be easily recognized by its stout stem, thick, fleshy, lance-shaped leaves, obscurely triple-ribbed, and showy flowers, which, however, are not nearly so yellow as those of *S. nemoralis*, nor as beautiful. It is common from Maine to Virginia.

S. bicolor is a white or cream-colored variety; my drawing shows how it looks in nine cases out of ten. It is a very common sort to me, as it is plentiful in the White Mountain region; but there are many localities where its whitish flowers are rarely seen. So unlike is it to the popular notion of golden-rod that, upon picking a specimen one time and telling its name to an inquiring friend who was walking with me, the surprised response came: "What! that thing golden-rod? Nonsense!" There is just a slight resemblance in the superficial appearance of the flower to mignonette.

S. Lanceolata.

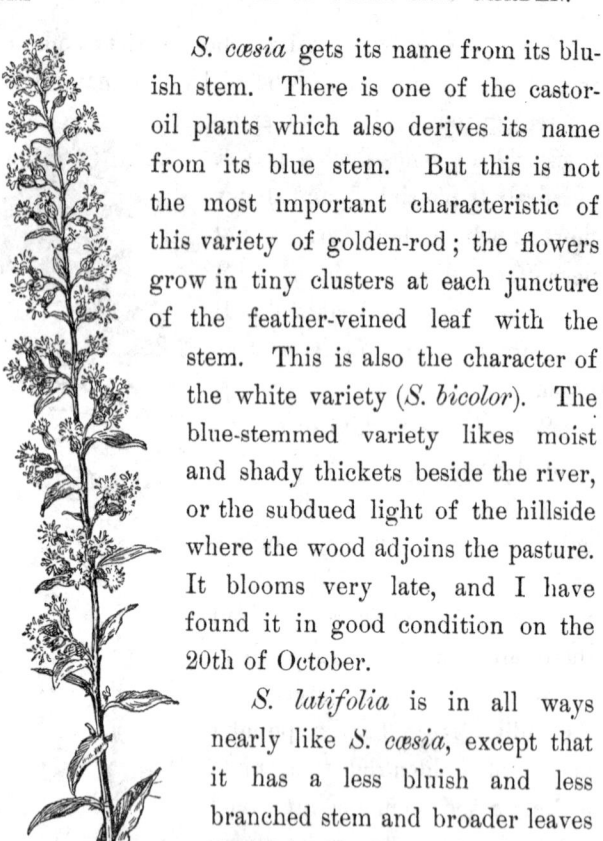

S. cæsia gets its name from its bluish stem. There is one of the castor-oil plants which also derives its name from its blue stem. But this is not the most important characteristic of this variety of golden-rod; the flowers grow in tiny clusters at each juncture of the feather-veined leaf with the stem. This is also the character of the white variety (*S. bicolor*). The blue-stemmed variety likes moist and shady thickets beside the river, or the subdued light of the hillside where the wood adjoins the pasture. It blooms very late, and I have found it in good condition on the 20th of October.

S. latifolia is in all ways nearly like *S. cæsia*, except that it has a less bluish and less branched stem and broader leaves sharply toothed; the three or four rays of the little flowers are bright yellow. It is common northward in shaded places, and south along the mountains.

S. Bicolor.

S. odora (sweet golden-rod) has

fragrant leaves without toothed edges, which slightly remind one of the odor of anise, and are shiny and well formed, but the flowers are not particularly attractive. It yields a volatile oil. I found this variety common in the "Pines" of New Jersey. It generally grows on the edges of thickets in dry, sandy soil.

S. speciosa is not quite as common as some of the other varieties, but it is very handsome. It grows from three to six feet high, has large, dark-green, slightly toothed leaves, and its ample panicle of bloom, formed by a number of erect flower stems (racemes), is bright golden yellow. The little blossom when placed under the glass shows five or more good-sized yellow rays. The stem of this variety is very stout and smooth.

S. Cæsia.

These fourteen varieties are commonly met with from Maine southward to the pine barrens of New Jersey. It must be remembered that there are in all about seventy varieties. There is always a preponderance of a certain variety in a particular locality—for instance, beside the road running parallel with the river in Campton there is a great quantity of the white-flowered variety and little or no *S. rugosa*. This last-mentioned flower is commoner in several meadow copses beside the river than any of the varieties which Gray mentions as the very commonest. The golden-rod is certainly our representative American wild flower. Not many years ago, when the subject of a national flower became interesting, Mr. Louis Prang, of Boston, published a little tract suggesting the arbutus and golden-rod as competitors for the position of honor, and requested an expression of choice from the people. The response was decisive; and the vote was cast by an overwhelming majority for the golden-rod.

S. Speciosa.

Golden-Rod gone to Seed.

226 FAMILIAR FLOWERS OF FIELD AND GARDEN.

Aster, or Starwort.
Aster.

There are between forty and fifty species of wild asters in our country, so I can only draw attention to the commoner ones. Most of these have a distinct individuality, which it will be impossible for one to mistake who will closely follow the descriptions:

A. ericoides bears such tiny white flowers that there is no possibility of confusing it with any other common aster; it is enough to know that the little white rays are like hairs in fineness, and the yellow centers are compact like those of the daisy—in fact, the flower looks like a miniature daisy, and would never be taken for an aster by one whose acquaintance with wild flowers is slight. This variety grows about two feet high, has slender, wiry stems, and small, narrow, plain-looking leaves. It is found in partially shady, or open and dry places, and blooms from midsummer until late in October. I

A. Ericoides.

have found this aster as early as July 8th in the wayside places of Campton.

A. Tradescanti is a smooth variety, slender-stemmed, with small, lance-shaped leaves, and very small white flowers *closely* encircling the upper side of the flowering branches.

A. paniculatus is a variety taller than *A. Tradescanti*, with pale violet-tinted or white flowers. Its stem is much branched, and bears narrow lance-shaped leaves tapering at the end; those below are sharply toothed. This variety and *A. Tradescanti* grow in wet situations.

A. patens, sometimes called spreading aster, is common about the middle of August beside the road and on the edge of thickets, and usually on dry ground, but without a sunny exposure. The center of the flower is greenish yellow,

A. Patens.

and the rays are purple with quite a curvature; the leaf has an elongated heart-shape and grows close to the stem. The flower grows singly on a very thin stem which bears a few little leaflets. The main stem, which is about two feet high, is covered below with very minute short hairs.

A. Novæ Angliæ, the New England aster, is common everywhere, and grows taller than the preceding variety; perhaps its stem reaches an average height of five feet. The flower is a trifle smaller than that of *A. patens*, but it bears many more purple rays; sometimes these are magenta-purple. A large flower cluster terminates the coarse, hairy stem which is covered to the very end with lance-shaped, dark-green leaves. This variety frequents wet meadows, and blooms about the middle or the end of August.

A. Novæ Angliæ.

A. cordifolius is a small-flowered variety, whose blue-lavender rays and variable (sometimes reddish, sometimes purplish) little flower centers are the best means, in my opinion, for its identification. The stem is very much branched above, and these branches bear numerous flower clusters; the leaves are sharp-pointed, heart-shaped, and have slender little stems. This variety is common in woodlands and on the sloping banks of the highway. It likes a partially shaded locality, and blooms early and late.

A. undulatus, or the wavy-leafed aster, is common on the edge of woodlands, and in the pastures. The flowers, about as large as a silver quarter, are lavender-purple with purple-edged yellow

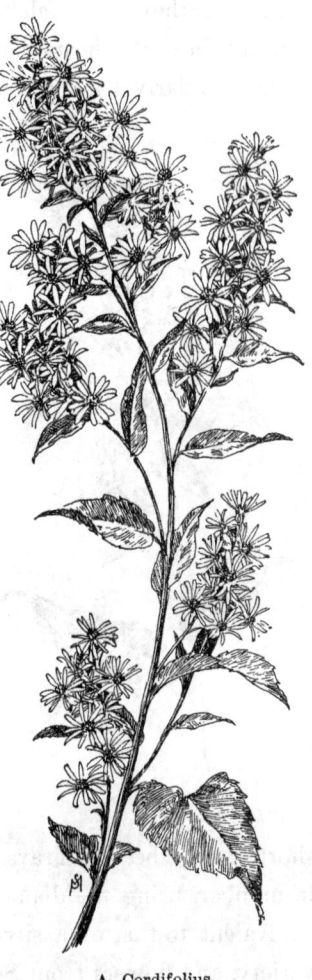

A. Cordifolius.

230 FAMILIAR FLOWERS OF FIELD AND GARDEN.

centers. The wavy-edged leaves have a variety of forms as they grow along the reddish stem; the lowest ones are heart-shaped, and the upper ones have singularly flaring stems which clasp the main stalk of the plant; and those which adjoin the flower stems are small and sharply pointed. This variety flowers early in August.

A. spectabilis is one of the prettiest of the Aster family, although its flower heads are few. It grows along the coast between New Hampshire and New Jersey, where the sandy soil is quite to its liking. The flower rays are bright purple and nearly an inch long; although in many instances much shorter, these beautiful rays, perhaps sixteen to twenty in number, bring the diameter of the flower to a size equivalent to that of a silver dollar. This is a late variety, and flowers from September to November.

A. Undulatus.

A. longifolius grows about three feet high, has lance-shaped leaves, which are firm and glossy, and a

A. Spectabilis.   A. Longifolius.

characteristic flower envelope (involucre), which has many little, curled-over, leaflike scales; the flowers, which are about as large as a half dollar, are light violet. The leaves of this aster are remarkably long; some of the largest, although narrow, reach a length of four inches. It grows in low grounds, and blooms in September and October.

232 FAMILIAR FLOWERS OF FIELD AND GARDEN.

China Aster.
Callistephus Chinensis.

The botanical name of the cultivated aster is from two Greek words meaning beautiful crown. The flower comes to us from China and Japan. There are so many varieties that I can only mention those of prominent type. The Victoria is an old favorite, whose flowers, in a great variety of colors, are soft-rayed and have a reflex curve. Truffaut's aster is incurved and has a large range of colors. Betteridge's quilled aster has distinct quills or needles, and is a flower of German fame; in this variety there is a flower perfectly yellow in tint which I have obtained from Mr. W. Atlee Burpee, of Philadelphia. A yellow aster seems an anomaly; but there is no question about the color of this particular flower, whose basic tone is white, stained lemon-yellow. The Triumph is a variety with brilliant red flowers. One of the most beautiful newer varieties is the Comet. This is a flower with reflex curling

Comet Aster.

rays, of a singularly translucent quality of color. The white ones are particularly delicate and altogether lovely. There are many new varieties of the aster, but they do not diverge very greatly from the types already mentioned.

The flower blooms in late summer and early autumn; the varieties forced to bloom in midsummer can not be considered perfectly satisfactory. True blue is not a color peculiar to the flower, and those varieties named blue are, as a rule, strongly saturated with purple; nor is there a scarlet aster; any flower so called is most likely pure red with a crimson cast.

CHAPTER XVI.

SEPTEMBER AND NOVEMBER.

Iron-weed to Chrysanthemum.

Iron-weed.
Vernonia Noveboracensis.

THE iron-weed has a formidable Latin name, which in plain English means Mr. Vernon, and "belonging to New York," but this fact does not confine the weed to the boundaries of this State. It grows all along the coast country, beside the river and the road, anywhere from three to five feet high; so it must surely be seen by the most unobserving. Its rather sparing cluster of crimson-magenta flowers shows itself about the time of the asters, and it might easily be mistaken

Iron-weed.

for a variety of the latter flower. But my drawing shows that it is a very different character; the flowers are formed remotely like bachelors' buttons, and have a tubular character, with the involucre (flower envelope) covered with short bristles of a rusty-brown color. The plant was named for Mr. Vernon, an early English botanist. It blooms in August and September. *V. altissima* is a tall variety with large flowers which grows west and south of Pennsylvania.

Bitter-sweet. Bitter-sweet is a beautiful, climbing,
Celastrus scandens. twining shrub with which every one ought to be familiar who travels over the country road in early fall when the scarlet berries are revealed inside of the open orange-colored pods with charming effect amid the autumnal foliage. These pretty berries conjure up thoughts of Dr. Holland's poem entitled Bitter-sweet, and, may I be permitted to add, sweet cider. Although the climbing shrub with its beautiful berry clusters is a familiar sight beside the cider mills of New Jersey, it has no connection, direct or implied, with that famous beverage known as "Jersey lightning" which, about the time that the berries appear, is being distilled from the juice of the ubiquitous and innocent apple; so we must hope that the cider mentioned in the poem did not have the remarkable strength attributed to this New Jersey product.

Garget.
Phytolacca decandra.

In September the handsome purple berries of the garget plant appear, hanging their dark clusters against the hazy olive foliage of early autumn. In summer the rather inconspicuous white flowers, which grow on slender stems and somewhat resemble the white lilac, are not apt to attract notice; but the berries are really beautiful and do not fail to catch the eye. The name *Phytolacca* is a combination of an incorrect Greek word for plant with the French word *lac* (lake), which was derived from the crimson character of the berry juice. The juice has been used for coloring purposes, but unsuccessfully, as it fades. Garget reaches a height of from six to nine feet, and grows in the thickets where the ground is low.

Garget.

Closed or Bottle Gentian.
Gentiana Andrewsii.

The closed or bottle gentian is an inhabitant of the woods northward. Its flowers are like tiny thick tenpins in shape, and are often a very good blue. The blue flower, however, is a creation of the imagination; in reality it does not exist, and the so-called blue is often a decided *violet* of dilute character;

this is the case with the violet, harebell, aster, and blue-eyed grass. But the bottle gentian often shows a decided pale violet blue color, which comes within the category of blues; however, I can not see the same blue in the flower that Thoreau talks about; he says, "a splendid blue, . . . bluer than the bluest sky." Now, if we will look at that part of the heavens which is exactly at right angles with the position held by the sun on a clear day, we will see a color which Ruskin calls "blue fire." If a piece of white paper is held up so that it receives

Closed Gentian.

the full sunlight and is in juxtaposition with the blue sky, it will be seen that the sky-blue is as brilliant as the white paper. This is a revelation which, to say the least, is surprising. By no possibility can we obtain a *blue* color which is as bright as white, either in the paint box or on the flower petal. So those who, like Thoreau and Bryant, tell us about flowers as blue as the sky, must be allowed a certain latitude in their descriptions, as these are often poetic without being scientifically true. The bottle gentian, then, is so purplish that we can only call it blue by sufferance; one moment's comparison of the flower with the blue sky will prove this beyond question. Not only in the White Mountains, but in Pennsylvania, it is one of the latest fall flowers. Southern Europe has two splendid varieties of the gentian, colored about as blue as a flower can well be—*G. Alpina*, which is cup-shaped or vase-shaped with a pointed edge, and *G. verna*, which is a charming deep blue; the flower cup has five round petal-like divisions. Also, a flower of the Pyrenees shows a good blue (*Delphinium peregrinum*), but this is not as blue as the last-mentioned gentian. There is quite a difference of opinion among botanists as to whether the closed gentian is subject to cross-fertilization, or simply fertilizes itself; Gray thought the former was the case, and says that he has seen a bumblebee force its way into the corolla; but Dr. Kunze concludes that the flowers derive no aid from insects. This

SEPTEMBER AND NOVEMBER. 239

only shows how much there is yet to be learned about a common wild flower.

Fringed Gentian. The beautiful fringed gentian must
Gentiana crinita. ever be associated in one's mind with the poet Bryant, who has written such charming lines on it. To him it was the flower of hope which comes

"When . . .
 . . . shortening days portend
 The aged year is near his end,"

and with sweet and quiet eye looks through its fringes heavenward; and he thought it was as blue as the sky. But the blue of the flower is not as true as its expression of hopeful dependence; there is indeed a marvelous heavenward-looking calmness expressed by every one of its lines. The

Fringed Gentian.

stem and corolla are both perpendicular, and the "fringed lids" are spread out horizontally like the extended palms of one who stands a supplicant before Heaven. The flower cup is about two inches long and has four divisions, which turn back flatly at the top; these divisions are opened or closed according to the brightness or dullness of the day. If a burst of sunshine occurs on a dull day the flower expands in a very few minutes. It always closes at night, and it will not open the next day if the sun does not shine. It can by no means be called common; I have found it in the vicinity of Boston and in one or two localities on Long Island, but I have never succeeded in finding it in the Pemigewasset Valley. It belongs generally in low grounds, throughout our country, North and West. As it is presumably a biennial plant, one must not be surprised if it is not found year after year in the same spot. Prof. Meehan expresses the opinion that the length of its life is still uncertain, and he says, "Even now the only certain point is that it dies after flowering." The time to look for the flower is in October; and S. R. Bartlett says:

> "I know not why, but every sweet October
> Down the fair road that opens to the sea,
> Dear in the wayside grasses tinging sober,
> Blooms my blue gentian faithfully for me."

SEPTEMBER AND NOVEMBER. 241

Fall Dandelion.
Leontodon autumnalis.

The autumn or fall dandelion is not nearly so beautiful as its spring relative, as it is lacking in both the size and rich color of the latter flower. Still, the little yellow blossom is pretty, and it is common over hillside pastures and sandy meadows from July until November. Its flower stem is bare, long, and scrawny-looking, and has what appears like tiny scales (bracts) regularly arranged quite a distance downward from the flower. The leaves, similar to those of the spring dandelion, but blunt-toothed, are very small and grow close to the ground. I found this flower plentifully scattered over the

Leontodon Autumnalis.

Clarendon hills south of Boston, but never found many well developed specimens in the Pemigewasset Valley or among the White Hills. In the southwesterly States, from Maryland to Kansas and Texas, there is another flower which closely resembles this fall dandelion, called the Cynthia dandelion;* this variety may be easily distinguished from the other, as it has *naked* flower stems (without the tiny bracts), and the lower leaves are sharp-toothed; there are also long, very narrow, straight leaves, peculiar to this Cynthia dandelion, which will not be found in either of the other varieties. But the Cynthia stops blooming just about the time the fall dandelion begins; so there is small chance of one flower being mistaken for the other.

Nightshade.
Solanum Dulcamara.

About the time when the fall dandelion is blooming and the latest fringed gentian flowers close their eyes to the slanting sun of October we may see the thickets which flank the roads just outside of Boston covered with beautiful elliptical red berries, which hang in graceful clusters from the thin protruding branches. These berries possess exactly the same translucent quality of color as the red cherry does—a pure red without a

---

* Its botanical name is both *Cynthia dandelion* and *Krigia dandelion;* the latter is given the preference in Gray's Manual, revised edition.

trace of scarlet. Thoreau was keenly appreciative of color, which he often accurately described; he says, alluding to the nightshade berries: "I do not know

Nightshade.

any clusters more graceful and beautiful than these drooping cymes of scented or translucent, cherry-colored elliptical berries." The tall, climbing, woody stems are covered with dull, bluish-green, sharp-pointed, heart-shaped leaves with variations like my sketch, by which one may easily identify the shrub. It grows in moist ground, and came to this country from Europe. It is common in the proximity of our cities, but I have rarely found it in the

Halbert Three-lobed Leaf.

Pemigewasset Valley, and then only beside some old homestead. The little purple flowers grow in small clusters, and appear in summer. It is curious to learn that the nightshade is closely related to the potato (*S. tuberosum*), the eggplant (*S. melongena*), and the pretty ornamental little shrub called Jerusalem cherry (*S. Pseudo-Capsicum*). A comparison of the flowers of these plants will reveal the relationship by their similarity.

Winterberry, or Black Alder.
Ilex verticillata.

At the very close of the season of flowers in autumn our attention will be attracted to the brilliant scarlet berries of the black alder which dot its gray stems and cling to them long after the leaves have dropped. The leaves are light green, sharp-pointed, and elliptical in shape, and have a fine-toothed edge; they are two inches long. The shrub is certainly very decorative, and one wishes it were a little more common; but while it is plentiful in some localities, it is quite absent in others, and disappointing on that account. The smooth winterberry (*I. lævigata*) has longer, narrower leaves, shining above, and long-peduncled sterile flowers; the smooth alder (*Alnus serrulata*) must not be confused with either of the

Black Alder.

foregoing species; it is a member of the Birch family, and bears a calkin, like my sketch, in early spring. It is not surprising to learn that the black alder is a near relative of the English holly (*I. Aquifolium*), to which it bears a slight resemblance; but the holly has that bold, spiny leaf which gives it an additional charm. Our own holly (*I. opaca*) is a tree nearly forty feet high, growing in New England and southward, with oval, wavy-margined, spiny-toothed, evergreen leaves, and red berries. It is not as beautiful as the English holly. The so-called mountain holly (*Nemopanthes fasicularis*) is not a true holly at all; its berries are a deep red, with a dull surface. It is common in the wet bogs northward, particularly in the White Mountain district.

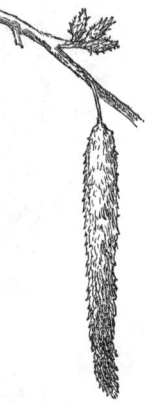

Smooth Alder Catkin.

Cosmos.
Cosmos bipinnatus.

Cosmos is a beautiful white (or pale-pink) flower which closely resembles coreopsis or the single dahlia in form, and blooms in early autumn. It is an annual which grows six feet high sometimes, and its only enemy in the North is Jack Frost, who appears too early in New Hampshire for me to grow the plant successfully in my garden. The dainty white flower comes to us from

Mexico, and grows wild there as well as in Texas; it thrives better, therefore, in the gardens of the South. The variety called Pearl is considered the best. The flower is cultivated by the florists, and is seen in great luxuriant clusters in their store windows in New York and Boston during the winter. The Texan ladies who visit Washington wonder why we value a flower which is a common weed in their native State. But "a prophet is not without honor save in his own country," and the only fault of cosmos is, it happens to be too *common* in Mexico and Texas. For us it is the dearest and the last flower of autumn, excepting the chrysanthemum.

Cosmos.

Chrysanthemum.
Chrysanthemum Indicum.

The chrysanthemum is an Oriental flower, which comes to us from Japan and China; indirectly some of the smaller varieties come from England and France. But the florists have taken almost complete possession of the flower, and as their hothouse blooms are perfectly huge as well as gorgeous in color, our garden varieties suffer by comparison and are consequently neglected. The Chrysanthemum family is immense, and numbers something like four hundred distinct varieties; this number is constantly being added to by newer hybrids. But these florists' chrysanthemums are not hardy; they are mostly of the Japanese class; it is the older Chinese varieties which stand the cold of our Northern winters best. The pompon variety is quite as hardy as any sturdy-going perennial. In this class there are Alba perfecta, white; Gaillardia, brown and yellow mixed; Golden Circle, golden orange; Bob, crimson; and Rubra perfecta, magenta. Of the hardy Chinese class there are: Diana, white; King of the Crimsons, deep crimson; George Glenny, yellow; and Dr. Brock, golden yellow. These varieties are recommended by Mr. John Saul, who is an authority on such matters, and I can testify to the excellence of his judgment. The King of the Crimsons I consider one of the finest of the dark red, hardy chrysanthemums. One of the most beautiful flowers of the anemone class is Princess; it is white.

Pompon Chrysanthemum.

In our more southern gardens these varieties will be found blooming as late as Christmas, if December should be mild.

The chrysanthemum is indeed the last and most beautiful autumn flower of all Flora's train; and whatever we may say of the rose, we must acknowledge the lovely Golden Flower *another* queen—the Queen of Autumn. When the summer flowers are gone and the birds have flown southward; when the chill winds come down from the icy regions of the North, when there are no leaves, no blue sky—

" No t'other side the way "—

then comes our Autumn Queen, and fills our laps with a wealth of bloom the like of which we never saw in June. Oliver Wendell Holmes sweetly sings about the Golden Flower as though she were an angel queen:

> " The fields are stripped, the groves are dumb;
>   The frost-flowers greet the icy moon—
> Then blooms the bright chrysanthemum.
>
> " The stiffening turf is white with snow,
>   Yet still its radiant disks are seen
> Where soon the hallowed morn will show
>   The wreath and cross of Christmas green;
> As if in autumn's dying days
>   It heard the heavenly song afar,
> And opened all its glowing rays,
>   The herald lamp of Bethlehem's star.
>
> .   .   .   .   .   .

SEPTEMBER AND NOVEMBER.

"Thy smile the scowl of winter braves,
　　Last of the bright-robed, flowery train,
Soft sighing o'er the garden graves:
　　'Farewell! farewell!—we meet again!'
So may life's chill November bring
　　Hope's golden flower, the last of all,
Before we hear the angels sing
　　Where blossoms never fade and fall!"

A SYSTEMATICAL INDEX

OF THE NAMES, COLORS, AND LOCALITIES OF
FAMILIAR FLOWERS OF THE UNITED STATES,
INCLUDING A FLORAL CALENDAR.

The names with the asterisk (*) are those of flowers not mentioned in this book. The letter on the right of each common name is the initial of the botanical name (or *vice versa*), also in this index.

252 FAMILIAR FLOWERS OF FIELD AND GARDEN.

SPECIES AND VARIETIES.	Family.	Color.	Locality.	Environment.	Time of bloom.	Pages.
Acanthus						147
Achillea millefolium (see Yarrow)						175
Aconite, A.	Crowfoot.	Dark violet.	Pa. and S. in mts. Wisc.	Rich, shady soil.	June–Sept.	196
Aconitum uncinatum (see Aconite).						196
Acorus Calamus (see Sweet Flag).						74
Actæa alba (see Baneberry, White).						27
Actæa spicta (var. rubra), (see Baneberry, Red).						
Adder's-Tongue, E.	Lily.	Light and russet yellow.	N. E. to Fla., W. to Minn. and Ark.	Rich ground.	Apr., May.	9
*Ageratum Mexicanum	Composite.	Lilac and blue lilac.	From trop. America, gardens.	Light soil.	June–Sept.	244
*Agrimony, A.	Rose.	Yellow.	Common.	Fields and borders of woods.	July–Sept.	244
*Agrimonia Eupatoria (see Agrimony).						
Alder, Black, I.	Holly.	White.	Common.	Low ground.	May, June.	244
Alder, Smooth (see Alnus).						
*Alisma Plantago (see Water-Plantain).						
Alnus serrulata, A.	Birch, div. Oak.	Rusty yellowish.	Mass. to Minn. Tex., and southward.	Borders of streams, swamps.	Apr.	244
Althæa officinalis (see Marsh-Mallow)						192
Althæa rosea (see Hollyhock)						192
Althæa, Shrubby, H.	Mallow.	Purple, pink, and white.	From the Levant, old gardens.	Good soil.	Aug., Sept.	194
Alyssum maritimum (see Sweet Alyssum)						89
Amaranth (see Amarantus)						121
Amarantus caudatus (see Prince's Feather)						121
Amarantus Gangeticus or melancholicus (see Love-lies-Bleeding).						121

A SYSTEMATICAL INDEX.

Name	Family	Color	Range	Soil	Time	Page
Amarantus hypochondriacus	Amaranth.					121
Amarantus retroflexus (see Pigweed)						121
Amaryllis Atamasco (see Zephyranthes and Atamasco Lily).						107
*American Cowslip, D.	Primrose.	White, purple, and violet.			May, June.	
Ampelopsis quinquefolia (see Virginia-Creeper)						138
Anaphalis margaritacea (see Everlasting, Pearly).						185
*Andromeda ligustrina	Heath.	White.	N. Y. and N. E. to Fla. and Ark.	Wet grounds.	May, June.	
Andromeda Mariana (see Stagger-bush).						84
Anemone nemorosa (see Anemone, Wood).						16
*Anemone Putens (var. Nuttalliana), P.	Crowfoot.	Purplish.	Ill. and Mo.	Plains.	Mar., Apr.	
Anemomella thalictroides (see Anemone, Rue).						34, 159
Anemone, Rue, T. A.	Crowfoot.	White.	Common.	Woods.	Apr., May.	17, 34
*Anemone Virginiana, A.	Crowfoot.	Greenish.	Common.	Woods and meadows.	June–Aug.	
*Anemone, Virginian (see Anemone Virginiana).						16, 72
Anemone, Wood, A.	Crowfoot.	White.	Common.	Woods.	Apr., May.	14
Antennaria plantaginifolia (see Everlasting, Early).						
Antirrhinum majus (see Snapdragon)	Figwort.	Purple and violet.	From Texas and Mexico, gardens.	Good soil.	July, Aug.	174
Antirrhinum maturandioides						174
Antirrhinum Orontium	Figwort.	Lilac-purple.	Common in waste grounds and old gardens.	Light soil.	July, Aug.	174
Apocynum androsæmifolium (see Dogbane)						160
Aquilegia Canadensis (see Columbine)						54
Aralia nudicaulis (see Sarsaparilla, Wild)						133
*Aralia quinquefolia (see Ginseng).						

254 FAMILIAR FLOWERS OF FIELD AND GARDEN.

SPECIES AND VARIETIES.	Family.	Color.	Locality.	Environment.	Time of bloom.	Pages.
Aralia racemosa (see Spikenard).						
Aralia trifolia (see Ground Nut).						
Arbutus, Trailing, E.	Heath.	Pink.	N. E. to Minn. S. to Fla. and Ky.	Sandy woods, by rocks.	Apr., May.	1, 9, 82
Arctium Lappa (see Burdock).						97
Arenaria Grœnlandica (see Sandwort).						65, 66
Arethusa bulbosa	Orchis.	Magenta-pink.	N. E. to mts. in N. C., W. to Ind. and Minn.	Bogs.	May–July.	
Argemone (var. Albiflora)	Poppy.	White.	From Mexico and trop. America, gardens.	Light soil.	June–Aug.	149
Argemone Mexicana (see Prickly Poppy, Yellow)						142, 146
Arisæma triphyllum (see Jack-in-the-Pulpit)						42
Aristolochia Sipho (see Dutchman's Pipe).						
Arrowhead, S.	Water Plantain.	White.	Common.	Water or wet ground.	June–Aug.	75
Asarum Canadense (see Wild Ginger).						162
Asclepias Cornuti (see Milkweed).						164
Asclepias tuberosa (see Butterfly-weed).						
Ascyrum Crux-Andreæ (see St. Andrew's Cross)						
Aster cordifolius	Composite.	Pale lavender-blue.	Very common.	Shady banks and woodlands.	Sept., Oct.	228
Aster ericoides	Composite.	White.	N. E. to Minn. and southward.	Dry, open places.	July–Oct.	226
Aster linarii folius	Composite.	Violet-blue.	Common.	Open places. sandy soil.	Sept., Oct.	
Aster longifolius	Composite.	Lighter violet.	North N. E. to Minn.	Low grounds.	Sept., Oct.	231
Aster Novæ Angliæ	Composite.	Red-magenta and violet-purple.	Common.	Moist grounds.	Aug.–Oct.	228, 237

A SYSTEMATICAL INDEX.

Name	Family	Color	Range	Habitat	Time	Page
Aster paniculatus	Composite.	Pale lilac and white.	Common.	Moist. shady places.	Sept., Oct.	227
Aster patens	Composite.	Violet-purple.	Mass. to Minn. and southward.	Dry ground.	Aug.-Oct.	227
Aster spectabilis	Composite.	Bright violet.	Mass. to Del., near coast.	Sandy soil.	Sept.-Nov.	230
Aster Tradescanti	Composite.	Purplish and white.	Mass. to Minn. and S. to Va. and Ill.	Moist, low grounds.	Sept., Oct.	227
Aster undulatus	Composite.	Violet-blue.	Common.	Dry copses.	Aug.-Oct.	229
Aster, Betteridge's Quilled	....	....	....	....	....	232
Aster, China, C	Composite.	Various.	From China and Japan, gardens.	Rich soil.	Aug.-Oct.	204, 232
Aster, Comet	....	....	....	....	....	232
*Aster, Golden (see Chrysopsis).						
Aster, Traffaut's	....	....	....	....	....	232
Aster, Triumph	....	....	....	....	....	232
Aster, Victoria	....	....	....	....	....	232
Aster, Yellow	....	....	....	....	....	232
Atamasco Lily, A. Z.	Amaryllis.	White and pink.	Pa., Va., to Fla., and gardens.	Low, dry ground.	Mar.-June.	107
*Atropa Belladonna (see Belladonna).						
*Avens, Water, G.	Rose.	Purplish orange.	N. E. to N. J., W. to Minn. and Mo.	Bogs and wet meadows.	May-July.	60
*Azalea calendulacea (see Flame-colored A.).						
Azalea nudiflora (see Purple or Pink A.).						
*Azalea viscosa (see Clammy A.).						
*Azalea, Clammy, A. R.	Heath.	White, pale pink.	Can. and Me. to Fla. and Ark.	Swamps near coast.	June, July.	
*Azalea, Flame-colored, A. R.	Heath.	Orange to orange-red.	Mts. of Pa. to Ga.	Woods.	May.	
Azalea, Purple or Pink, A. R.	Heath.	Flesh-color, pink, and purple.	N. E. to Fla., Ill., Mo., and Tex.	Swamps.	Apr., May.	60

FAMILIAR FLOWERS OF FIELD AND GARDEN.

SPECIES AND VARIETIES.	Family.	Color.	Locality.	Environment.	Time of bloom.	Pages.
Bachelor's Button, C.	Composite.	Various.	From Europe, gardens.	Light soil.	June–Sept.	90, 235
Balsam, I.	Geranium.	Various.	From India, gardens.	Light soil.	July–Sept.	116, 119, 172
Balsam, Malmaison.						116
*Baneberry, Red, A.	Crowfoot.	White.	Common, northward.	Rich woods.	Apr., May.	
Baneberry, White, A.	Crowfoot.	White.	Common.	Rich woods.	Apr., May.	27, 191
*Baptisia tinctoria (see Indigo, Wild).						
*Barbarea vulgaris (see Winter Cress).						
Bedstraw, Sweet-scented (see Galium triflorum)						
Bee-balm (see Oswego Tea).						
Beggar-ticks, B.	Composite.	Rusty greenish.	Common.	Moist, waste places.	July–Oct.	186, 171
*Belladonna, A.	Night-shade.	Dull purple.	From Europe, gardens.	Good soil.	July, Aug.	185
*Bellis integrifolia (see Daisy, Western).						
Bellis perennis (see English Daisy).						
Bellwort, O.	Lily.	Cream-color.	N. E. to Fla., W. to Minn., Neb., and Ark.	Low woods.	Apr., May.	105, 106 15
Bessera elegans, C.	Lily.	Light orange-scarlet.	From Mexico, gardens.	Light soil.	July, Aug.	198, 202
*Betonica officinalis (see Betony).						
*Betony, S. B.	Mint.	Dull magenta.	From Europe, old gardens.	Good soil.	June–Aug.	186, 202
Bidens chrysanthemoides (see Bur-marigold, Larger).						
Bidens frondosa (see Beggar-ticks).						185
Bindweed, Field, C.	Convolvulus.	White or pinkish.	N. Atlantic States.	Old fields.	July, Aug.	134

A SYSTEMATICAL INDEX.

Bindweed, Hedge, C.	Convolvulus.			Alluvial soil, roadsides, etc.	July, Aug.	134
Bird's Nest (see Carrot).						181
Birthroot (see *Trillium erectum*).						22
Bishop's Cap (see Mitrewort, True).						26
Bitter-sweet, C.	Staff-tree.	Greenish cream-color.	Common.	Along streams, thickets.	June.	235
Black Alder (see Alder).						244
Black-eyed Susan (see *Rudbekia hirta*).						127
Black Scabiosa.						112, 207
Black Snakeroot, C.	Crowfoot.	White.	Me. to Wis., and southward.	Rich woods.	July.	28, 191
Bladder Campion (see Campion).						129
*Bladderwort (see *Utricularia vulgaris*).						
*Bladderwort, Large, U.	Bladderwort.	Yellow.	N. E. to Minn., S. to Va. and Tex., and westward.	Slow streams and ponds.	June-Aug.	152
Blanket Flower (see Gaillardia).						
Blazing-star, L.	Composite.	Magenta-purple.	N. E. Pa. to Minn. and southward.	Swampy ground and dry soil.	Aug., Sept.	90, 194
Bleeding-heart, D.	Fumitory.	Pink-red.	From N. China, gardens.	Good soil.	May, June.	19
Blood-root, S.	Poppy.	White.	Common.	Open, rich woods.	Apr., May.	12, 142
Bluebell, C.	Campanula.	Violet-blue, pale.	Common N. and S. in mts.	Rocky, shaded banks.	June-Sept.	165
*Blue Curls, T.	Trichostema.	Pale violet-blue.	E. Mass. to Ky., S. to Fla. and Tex.	Sandy fields.	Aug., Sept.	49, 237
Blue-eyed Grass, S.	Amaryllis.	Violet-blue.	Common.	Moist meadows, in the grass.	June-Aug.	73
Blue Flag, Larger (see Flag).						

SPECIES AND VARIETIES.	Family.	Color.	Locality.	Environment.	Time of bloom.	Pages.
Bluets, H............................	Madder.	White and bluish.	N. E. to Ga., W. to Mich. and Ala.	Moist and grassy ground.	Apr.-July.	48
Blue Vervain (see Vervain)........						
Blueweed (see Viper's Bugloss)...						132
Boneset, E..........................	Composite.	Dull, leaden white.	Common.	Meadows and low grounds.	Aug., Sept.	142, 195 213
Bouncing Bet, S....................	Pink.	Pale magenta-pink.	From Europe, gardens.	Roadsides.	July-Sept.	187
*Brachycome iberidifolia (see Swan River Daisy)						
Brassica nigra (see Mustard)......						
*Brooklime, American, V...........	Figwort.	Pale violet.	Common.	Brooks and ditches.	June-Aug.	83
Brunella vulgaris, S................	Mint.	Violet-purple.	Common.	Woods, roadsides, fields.	June-Oct.	167
*Buckwheat, Climbing False, P....	Buckwheat.	Greenish or pinkish-white.	Common.	Moist thickets.	June, July.	
Bugbane (see Black Snakeroot)....						
Bugloss, Small, L...................	Borage.	Light-blue.	N. E. to Va.	Dry, sandy fields.	June-Aug.	28 195
Bunch-berry, C.....................	Dogwood.	White.	N. E. to Ind. and Minn., far N. and W.	Damp, cold woods.	May, June.	81
*Burdock, A........................	Composite.	Magenta-purple.	From Europe, common.	Waste places and roadsides.	July-Oct.	
Bur-marigold, Larger, B...........	Composite.	Yellow.	Common.	Swamps.	Aug.-Oct.	186, 202
*Bush-clover, L.....................	Pulse.	Violet-purple.	Common.	Dry, sandy soil.	Aug., Sept.	
Bush-honeysuckle, D...............	Honeysuckle.	Honey-color.	N. E. to mts. of N. C., W. to Minn.	Rocky places, roadsides.	June-Aug.	96

A SYSTEMATICAL INDEX.

Name	Family	Color	Origin/Notes	Habitat	Season	Page
Butter and Eggs (see Toadflax)						173
Buttercup, Common, R.	Crowfoot.	Deeper yellow.	E. from Europe, W. native, common.	Low grounds.	June–Aug.	7, 102, 191
Buttercup, Early, R.	Crowfoot.	Deeper yellow.	Common.	Hills and rocky pastures.	Apr., May.	103
Butterfly Weed, A.	Milkweed.	Red-orange.	Common, southward.	Dry hills, pastures.	July, Aug.	164
Calamus (see Sweet Flag)						74
Calendula officinalis, P.	Composite.	Pale buff yellow to orange.	From Europe, gardens.	Sandy soil.	June–Nov.	7, 149
Calendula, Le Proust						150
Calendula, Meteor						150
Calendula, Prince of Orange						150
Calendula, Sulphur						150
Calendula, Trianon						85
Calico Bush (see *Kalmia latifolia*)						142
California Poppy (see Eschscholtzia)						6, 14, 132
Calla, Æthiopian, R.	Arum.	White.	From Cape of Good Hope, house and gardens.	Light soil.	Apr.–June.	
Calla, Little Gem						14
Calla palustris (see Water Arum)						132
Callistephus Chinensis (see Aster, China)						232
Calopogon pulchellus	Orchis.	Magenta or pink-purple.	N. E. to Fla. W. to Minn. and Mo.	Bogs.	June.	59
Caltha palustris (see Marsh Marigold)						6
Calystegia sepium or Convolvulus sepium (see Bindweed, Hedge).						134
Camassia Fraseri (see Wild Hyacinth)						5
Camellia Japonica						116
*Campanula Medium (see Canterbury Bells).						
Campanula rotundiflora (see Bluebell)						165

FAMILIAR FLOWERS OF FIELD AND GARDEN.

SPECIES AND VARIETIES.	Family.	Color.	Locality.	Environment.	Time of bloom.	Pages.
Campion, Bladder, S.	Pink.	White.	East N. E. to Ill.	Fields and roadsides.	June, July.	129
Campion, Starry, S.	Pink.	White.	R. I. to Minn. and southward.	Wooded banks.	June, July.	129
Canary-Bird Flower, T.	Geranium.	Pure yellow.	From S. America, gardens.	Light soil.	July-Sept.	115, 119
Candytuft, Dobbie's Spiral	Mustard.	Purple and white.	From Europe, gardens.			89
Candytuft, Garden, I.	Mustard.	Purple and white.	From Europe, gardens.			88, 88, 90
Candytuft, Rocket.				Light soil.	June-Sept.	89
*Canna Indica, I.	Banana.	Red and yellow.	Trop. America, gardens.			
*Canterbury Bells, C.	Campanula.	Pink, white, and violet-blue.	From Europe, gardens.	Light soil.	July-Sept.	
Capsella Bursa-Pastoris (see Shepherd's Purse).				Rich, light soil.	June-Aug.	
Caraway, C.	Parsley.	White.	Wild in the North, gardens.		June.	83
Cardinal Flower, L.	Lobelia.	Deep scarlet-red.	Common.	Fields and roadsides.	Aug.-Sept.	95, 96, 182
Carrot, Wild, D.	Parsley.	White.	From Europe, common.	Low ground.	June-Sept.	177, 183, 193
Carum Carui (see Caraway).				Wasteplaces, roadsides.		95, 181, 183
*Cassia Marilandica (see Senna).						95
*Castilleia coccinea (see Painted Cup).						
Castor-Oil Plant, R.	Spurge.	Ruddy greenish.	From Africa, gardens.	Sunny, rich soil.	Aug.	222
Catchfly, Night-flowering (see Silene Noctiflora).						128
* Catchfly, Sleepy (see Silene antirrhina).						
*Catchfly, Virginian (see Silene Virginica).						
Cat-Tail Flag, T.	Cat-tail.	Brown.	Common.	Marshes.	June, July.	
*Ceanothus Americanus (see New Jersey Tea).						

A SYSTEMATICAL INDEX.

Name	Family	Color	Range	Soil	Time	Page
Celastrus scandens (see Bitter-sweet)						235
Celosia cristata (see Cockscomb)						121
Centaurea Cyanus (see Bachelor's Button)						90
Centaurea moschata	Composite.		From Asia, gardens.	Light soil.	July-Sept.	91
Centaurea odorata (see Sweet Sultan)						91
Centaurea suaveolens						91
Centaurea candidissima (see Dusty Miller)						91
Centaurea Clementei (see Dusty Miller)						91
Centaurea gymnocarpa (see Dusty Miller)						91
Cerastium arvense (see Chickweed, Field Mouse-ear).						130
*Chamælirium, Carolinianum or luteum (see Devil's Bit).						
Checkerberry (see Wintergreen)						29
Chelone glabra (see Turtle-head)						157
Chickweed, Common, S	Pink.	White.	Common.	Damp grounds.	May-Aug.	131
Chickweed, Field Mouse-ear, C	Pink.	White.	Common.	Dry or rocky places.	May-July.	130
Chicory, C	Composite.	Violet-blue.	From Europe, N. E. to Iowa and Minn.	Waste places and road-sides.	July-Oct.	142, 183
Chimaphila maculata	Heath.	Flesh-color.	N. E. to Ga., W. to Minn. and Miss.	Dry woods.	June, July.	70
Chimaphila umbellata (see Pipsissewa)						70
*Chiogenes serphyllifolia (see Creeping Snow-berry).						
*Chocolate Root (see Avens, Water).						
Chrysanthemum, Alba perfecta						247
Chrysanthemum, Bob						247
Chrysanthemum Burridgeanum						154
Chrysanthemum, Diana						247
Chrysanthemum, Dr. Brock						247
Chrysanthemum, Gaillardia						247
Chrysanthemum, George Glenny						247

SPECIES AND VARIETIES.	Family.	Color.	Locality.	Environment.	Time of bloom.	Pages.
Chrysanthemum, Golden Circle						247
Chrysanthemum, Japanese and Chinese, C	Composite.	Various.	From China and Japan, gardens.	Rich soil.	Sept.-Dec.	105, 152, 246
Chrysanthemum, King of the Crimsons						247
Chrysanthemum, Princess						247
Chrysanthemum, Rubra perfecta						247
Chrysanthemum, Summer	Composite.	Yellow, red, white.	From the Levant, gardens.	Light soil.	June-Sept.	153
Chrysanthemum Coronarium (see Summer Chrysanthemum).						153
Chrysanthemum Indicum (see Chinese Chrysanthemum).						246
Chrysanthemum Leucanthemum (see Daisy, Oxeye).						105
Chrysanthemum parthenioides (see Feverfew).						106
Chrysanthemum Parthenium, P	Composite.	Crimson-pink and white.	Escaped from cultivation, gardens.	Roadsides and fields.	June, July.	105
Chrysanthemum roseum, P	Composite.	Pale red or pink.	From Persia, gardens.	Light soil.	June, July.	105
*Chrysopsis Mariana, A	Composite.	Golden yellow.	South N. Y. and Penn., southward near coast.	Dry barrens.	Aug.-Oct.	105
Cichorium Endivia (see Endive)						184
Cichorium Intybus (see Chicory)						183
Cimicifuga racemosa (see Black Snakeroot)						28
Cinquefoil, Common, P	Rose.	Yellow.	Common.	Grassy places and dry soil.	Apr.-Sept.	50, 77
Cinquefoil, Norway, P	Rose.	Yellow.	N. E. to N. J. W. to Minn. and Kan.	Waste places, roadsides.	July, Aug.	51
Cinquefoil, Shrubby, P	Rose.	Yellow.	N. E. to N. J. W. to Minn., Iowa, and northwest.	Wet grounds.	June-Sept.	52
Claytonia Virginica (see Spring Beauty)						18

*Cleavers, or Goose Grass (see Galium aparine).					
Clematis graveolens	Crowfoot.	Yellow.	From Thibet, gardens.	Good soil.	July, Aug.	139
Clematis Jackmanni	Crowfoot.	Light violet.	(A hybrid), gardens.	Good soil.	July, Sept.	140
Clematis paniculata	Crowfoot.	White.	From Japan, gardens.	Good soil.	July, Aug.	139
Clematis, Virginiana, V	Crowfoot.	Greenish-white.	Common.	Roadsides and river banks.	July, Aug.	138
Clematis Mme. Edouard Andre	Crowfoot.	Reddish.	Gardens.	Good soil.	July, Aug.	139
*Cleome pungens	Caper.	Crimson pink.	Mt. Carmel, Ill, and southward, gardens.	Waste grounds and ballast.	July, Aug.	42
Clintonia borealis	Lily.	Pale greenish yellow.	In mts. N. E. to N. C., W. to Minn.	Cold, moist woods.	June.	121
*Cnicus lanceolatus (see Thistle, Common).					
Cockscomb, C	Amaranth.	Various.	From India, gardens.	Light soil.	Aug., Sept.	121
*Collinsia bicolor	Figwort.	Violet-blue and white.	From California, gardens.	Good soil.	June-Aug.	
*Collinsia verna	Figwort.	Blue and white.	West N. Y. to W. Va., Wis., and Ky.	Moist soil.	May, June.	
*Collinsonia Canadensis (see Horse Balm).					
Columbine, Wild, A	Crowfoot.	Scarlet and yellow.	Common.	Beside rocks.	May-July.	54, 191, 196
Commelina Virginica, D	Mayaca.	Pale violet.	South N. Y. to Fla. W. to Mich, Iowa, and Mo.	Damp, rich woods and banks.	June-Aug.	100
*Compass-plant (see Rosin-weed).						127
Cone Flower (see Rudbekia hirta).						67
Convallaria majalis (see Lily-of-the-Valley).						134
Convolvulus arvensis (see Bindweed, Field).						82
Coptis trifolia (see Goldthread)						198
Coral Drops (see Bessera elegans)						

264 FAMILIAR FLOWERS OF FIELD AND GARDEN.

SPECIES AND VARIETIES.	Family.	Color.	Locality.	Environment.	Time of bloom.	Pages.
*Coral Root, C.	Orchis.	Purplish-brown.	N. E. to Ind., W. to Mo., Iowa, and Minn.	Dry woods.	July–Sept.	
*Corallorhiza multiflora (see Coral Root).						
Coreopsis auriculata	Composite.	Yellow.	Va. to Ill. and southward.	Rich woods and banks.	June–Sept.	202
Coreopsis coronata	Composite.	Maroon spot, yellow.	From Texas, gardens.	Light soil.	July, Aug.	201
Coreopsis Drummondii	Composite.	Maroon spot, yellow.	From Texas, gardens.	Light soil.	July, Aug.	186, 201, 245
Coreopsis lanceolata	Composite.	Yellow.	Mich. and Ill. to Va. and southward, and gardens.	Rich or damp soil.	June, July.	202
Coreopsis tinctoria	Composite.	Mixed deep-red and yellow.	Minn., Ark., Tex., and gardens.	Light soil.	July–Sept.	152, 201
*Corn Cockle, L.	Pink.	Red-purple.	From Europe, common.	In wheat fields.	June–Aug.	
Cornflower (see Bachelor's Button)						90
Cornus canadensis (see Bunch-berry)						81
*Cornus florida (see Dogwood. Flowering).						
*Cornus stolonifera (see Dogwood, Red-osier).						
Corpse Plant (see Indian Pipe)						
Cosmos bipinnatus	Composite.	White and pink.	From Mexico and Texas, gardens.	Good soil.	Sept.–Nov.	98
Cosmos, Pearl						245
Cotton, G.						246
Cowslip, English, P.	Primrose.	Yellow.	Gardens.	Rich soil.	Apr., May.	194
Cranberry, Large, V.	Heath.	Pink.	Northward, and N. C. to Minn.	Peat bogs.	June.	63

A SYSTEMATICAL INDEX.

Name	Family	Color	Location	Habitat	Month	Page
Cranesbill, Wild (see Geranium, Wild)						
*Creeping Snowberry, C.	Heath.	White.	N. E., N. J., Pa., to Minn. and northward, Alleghanies to N. C.	Mossy woods and peat bogs.	May.	77
*Crinkle Root, D.	Mustard.	White.	Me. to Minn. and Ky.	Rich woods.	May.	200
Crocus	Iris.	Various.	From Europe, gardens.	Grassy ground.	Apr., May.	
*Crotalaria sagittalis (see Rattlebox).						
Cuscuta Gronovii (see Dodder)						135
Cyclobothra flava	Lily.	Russet, golden yellow.	Oregon and Cal., gardens.	Good ground.	June-Sept.	199
Cynthia Dandelion (see Dandelion, Cynthia).						104
Cypripedium acaule (see Moccason Flower, Pink).						56
Cypripedium parviflorum (see Lady's Slipper, Smaller Yellow).						
Cypripedium pubescens, L.	Orchis.	Pale yellow.	N. E. to Ga., W. to Minn. and E. Kan.	Bogs and low woods.	May, June.	58
*Cypripedium spectabile	Orchis.	Pink-magenta, and white.	Me., West N. E. to Minn. and Mo., S. to mts. of N. C.	Peat bogs.	July.	58
Daffodil, N.	Amaryllis.	Golden yellow.	From Europe, gardens.	Damp ground.	Apr., May.	108, 174
Dahlia variabilis	Composite.	Various.	From Mexico, gardens.	Rich, light soil.	Aug., Sept.	202, 245
Daisy, English (see English Daisy)						105
Daisy, Ox-eye, C.	Composite.	Yellow center, white.	From Europe, common E.	Fields and meadows.	June, July.	105
*Daisy, Western, B.	Composite.	Pale violet-purple.	Ky. and southwest.	Prairies and banks.	Mar.-June.	
Dandelion, Common, T.	Composite.	Rich golden yellow.	From Europe, common.	Pastures and fields.	Apr.-Sept.	103, 183, 241

SPECIES AND VARIETIES.	Family.	Color.	Locality.	Environment.	Time of bloom.	Pages.
Dandelion, Cynthia, K	Composite.	Golden yellow.	Md. to Kan., southward to Tex.	Moist ground.	Mar.-July.	104, 242
*Dandelion, Dwarf (see *Krigia Virginica*).						
Dandelion, Fall, L	Composite.	Golden yellow.	N. E. to Pa.	Meadows and roadsides.	July-Nov.	104, 241
Datura cornucopia						160
Datura Stramonium (see Thorn-Apple).						159
Daucus Carota (see Carrot).						181
Day-Flower, Common (see Commelina)						100
Day-Lily, Blue, F						79
*Day-Lily, Yellow, H	Lily.	Light violet-blue.	From Japan, gardens.	Good soil.	June-Aug.	
Delphinium Ajacis (see Larkspur, Rocket).	Lily.	Yellow.	From Europe, gardens.	Good soil.	June, July.	
Delphinium azureum	Crowfoot.	Blue and whitish.	Wis. to Dak., and southward.	Rich soil.	May, June.	191 191
Delphinium Consolida	Crowfoot.	Pale blue to pink, white.	Pa. to Va., and gardens.	Old grain fields.	July, Aug.	190
Delphinium elatum (see Larkspur, Bee).						190
Delphinium exaltatum	Crowfoot.	Violet and white.	Pa. to Minn., and southward.	Rich soil.	July, Aug.	191
Delphinium formosum	Crowfoot.	Light violet-blue.	Gardens.	Rich soil.	June, July.	190
Delphinium peregrinum						191, 288
Delphinium tricorne	Crowfoot.	Blue and white.	West Pa. to Minn. and southward.	Open woods.	Apr., May.	191
Dendromecon rigidum (see Poppy, Cal. Tree).						148
*Dentaria diphylla (see Crinkle-Root).						
*Devil's Bit, C	Lily.	Yellow.	N. E. to Ga., W. to Neb. and Ark.	Low grounds.	June.	
Dicentra Cucullaria (see Dutchman's Breeches)						19
Dicentra spectabilis (see Bleeding-Heart).						19
Diervilla Japonica	Honeysuckle.	Pink and white.	From Japan and China, gardens.	Good soil.	May.	97

A SYSTEMATICAL INDEX.

Name	Family	Color	Range	Habitat	Time	Page
Diervilla trifida (see Bush-Honeysuckle)						
Diplopappus linariifolius (see *Aster linariifolius*).						
Dipsacus sylvestris (see Teasel)						
Dodder, C.	Convolvulus.	White.	N. E. to Minn., S. to Fla. and Tex.	Wet, shady places.	June-Sept.	208
Dodecatheon Meadia (see American Cowslip).						135
Dogbane, Spreading, A.	Dogbane.	Pinky white.	Common.	Borders of thickets.	June, July.	160
*Dog's-Tooth Violet, White, E.	Lily.	Pinkish-white.	N. Y. to N. J., W. to Minn. and Ark.	Rich ground.	Apr., May.	
Dog's-Tooth Violet, Yellow (see Adder's Tongue)						9, 102
*Dogwood, Flowering, C.	Dogwood.	White and greenish.	S. N. E. to S. Minn., S. to Fla. and Tex.	Dry woods.	May, June.	
*Dogwood, Red-osier, C.	Dogwood.	White.	Common.	Wet places.	June.	
Draba verna (see Whitlow-Grass).						
Drosera filiformis (see Sundew, Thread-leaved).						
Drosera rotundiflora (see Sundew, Round-leaved).						
Dusty Miller, C.	Composite.	Purple.	From S. Europe, gardens.	Light soil.	Aug.	91
Dutchman's Breeches, D.	Fumitory.	White and pale yellow.	Common, westward.	Rich woods, leaf mold.	Apr., May.	19
*Dutchman's Pipe, A.	Birthwort.	Greenish or purplish.	Pa. to Ga., W. to Minn. and Kan.	Rich woods.	May.	
Dwarf Cornel (see Bunch-berry).						81
Dyer's Weed or Weld (see *Reseda luteola*).						91
Echium vulgare (see Viper's Bugloss)						195
Elderberry.						156
*Elecampane, I.	Composite.	Yellow.	From Europe, common.	Roadsides and damp pastures.	Aug.	
*Elodes campanulata (see St. John's-wort, Marsh).						

SPECIES AND VARIETIES.	Family.	Color.	Locality.	Environment.	Time of bloom.	Pages.
Endive, C.	Composite.	Lilac-blue.	From Europe, kitchen-gardens.	Light soil.	June–Aug.	184
English Daisy, B.	Composite.	Pink and white.	Rarely escaped from cultivation, gardens.	Grassy places.	May, June.	105, 106
Epigœa repens (see Arbutus)						1
Epilobium angustifolium (see Fireweed)						210
Erigeron bellidifolius (see Robin's Plantain)						47
*Erigeron Philadelphicum	Composite.	Pale magenta, flesh-color.	Common.	Moist grounds.	June–Aug.	
*Erythronium Albidum (see Dog's-Tooth Violet, White).						9
Erythronium Americanum (see Adder's Tongue, Yellow).						
Eschscholtzia Californica, P.	Poppy.	Yellow-white, yellow and orange.	California and gardens.	Light soil.	June–Sept.	142, 146, 147, 148, 149, 150
*Eucharidium concinnum	Evening-Primrose.	Magenta and white.	California and gardens.	Good soil.	June–Aug.	213
Eupatorium perfoliatum (see Boneset)						212
Eupatorium purpureum (see Joe-Pye Weed)						
*Euphorbia heterophylla (see Poinsettia of the United States).						
Euphorbia marginata (see Snow on the Mountain).						209
Euphorbia pulcherrima (see Poinsettia of Mexico).						
Evening-Primrose, O.	Evening-Primrose.	Yellow.	Common.	Open ground, roadsides.	June–Sept.	202, 210
Everlasting, Common, G.	Composite.	Yellowish-white.	Mostly north, common.	Pastures, fields, and woods.	June–Oct.	76, 77, 128 68, 185

A SYSTEMATICAL INDEX.

Name	Family	Color	Range	Habitat	Time	Page
Everlasting, Pearly, A............	Composite.	Pearly white.		Dry hills and woods.	Aug.	185
Everlasting, Spring or Early, A...	Composite.	Yellowish-white.	Common, northward. Common.	Sterile pastures, knolls, and banks.	Mar.–May.	14, 68
Fall Dandelion (see Dandelion, Fall)						
False Beech-drops, M..............	Heath.	Pinkish.	N. E. to Fla., W. to Ore.	Open pine woods.	June–Aug.	104, 100
False Mitrewort (see *Tiarella cordifolia*)..						
False Spikenard (see False Solomon's Seal).						25
False Solomon's Seal, S...........	Lily.	White.	N. E. to S. C., W. to Minn. E. Kan. and Tex.	Moist copses and thin woods.	May.	57 37
Feverfew, C	Composite.	White.	From China, gardens.	Light soil.	June–Sept.	106
Field Mouse-ear Chickweed (see Chickweed, Field Mouse-ear).						130
Fireweed, E........................	Evening Primrose.	Pale magenta.	N. E. and N. C., W. to Minn. and Kan. north and west.	Burned-over ground.	Aug., Sept.	210
*Flax, Red, L......................	Flax.	Crimson.	From the Levant, gardens.	Light soil.	Aug., Sept.	
Flag, Larger Blue, I...............	Iris.	Violet-blue.	N. E. to Fla., W. to Minn. and Ark.	Wet places.	May, June.	73
Fleur-de-lis (see Flag, Larger Blue).						73
Flowering Wintergreen (see *Polygala paucifolia*).						30
Foam-flower (see *Tiarella cordifolia*).						23, 25
Forget-me-not, M..................	Borage.	Light blue.	From Europe, escaped from cultivation, gardens.	Waste places. good soil.	June–Aug.	90, 183
*Four-o'clock, M...................	Four-o'clock.	Yellow, pink, white.	From trop. America, gardens.	Light soil.	June–Sept.	
*Foxglove, Downy False, G.........	Figwort.	Yellow.	N. E. to Wis., Iowa, S. to Ga. and Ark.	Open, dry woods.	Aug., Sept.	

SPECIES AND VARIETIES.	Family.	Color.	Locality.	Environment.	Time of bloom.	Pages.
*Foxglove, Smooth False, G	Figwort.	Yellow.	N. E. to Minn., S. to Fla. and Ill.	Rich, dry woods.	Aug., Sept.	51
Fragaria Indica (see Strawberry, Yellow-flowered).						52
Fragaria Virginiana (see Strawberry, Wild).						65
Fringed Orchis (see Orchis, Fringed-).						30
Fringed Polygala (see Polygala paucifolia).						79
Funkia ovata (see Day-Lily, Blue).						
Gaillardia amblyodon	Composite.	Deep red.	Gardens.	Light soil.	July, Sept.	152, 153
Gaillardia aristata	Composite.	Yellow and brown-purple.	N. Dak., west and southward, gardens.	Open ground.	July, Sept.	153
Gaillardia, Aurora Borealis						153
Gaillardia lanceolata	Composite.	Yellow and purplish.	S. Kan. to Tex. and Fla.	Open ground.	July, Aug.	153
Gaillardia Lorenziana	Composite.	Various.	Gardens.	Light soil.	July, Aug.	152
Gaillardia pulchella	Composite.	Dull red, yellow tips.	La. and westward, gardens.	Light soil.	July, Aug.	152, 153
Galanthus nivalis (see Snowdrop)						3
*Galium Aparine, C	Madder.	White.	Common.	Shady grounds.	June-Aug.	
Galium triflorum, B	Madder.	Greenish.	Common.	Rich woodlands.	June-Aug.	136
Garget, P	Pokeweed.	White.	Common.	Low grounds.	July-Sept.	235
Gaultheria procumbens (see Wintergreen)						29
*Gelsemium sempervirens (see Jessamine, Yellow).						

Gentian, Bottle or Closed, G.	Gentian.	White and light ultramarine-blue.	N. E. to Minn., S. to N. Ga.	Moist grounds.	Aug.-Oct.	157, 236
Gentian, Fringed, G.	Gentian.	Light ultramarine-blue.	N. E. to Dak., S. to Iowa, Ohio, and mts. to Ga.	Low grounds.	Sept., Oct.	239
Gentiana Alpina.						238
Gentiana Andrewsii (see Bottle Gentian).						236
Gentiana crinita (see Fringed Gentian).						239
Gentiana verna.						238
Geranium, Beauté Poitevine.						118
Geranium, Flowering, P.	Geranium.	Various.	From Cape of Good Hope, gardens.	Light soil.	May-Nov.	116
Geranium, Lady Washington (see Pelargoniums, cowled, heart-leaved, maple-leaved).						119, 200
Geranium, La Favorite.						118
Geranium maculatum (see Geranium, Wild).						77
Geranium, Madame Salleroi.						119
Geranium Robertianum (see Herb Robert).						79
Geranium, Wild, G.	Geranium.	Light purple.	Common.	Open woods and fields.	Apr.-July.	77, 119
Gerardia flava (see Foxglove, Downy False).						
Gerardia quercifolia (see Foxglove, Smooth False).						
Gerardia, Slender, G.	Figwort.	Magenta-purple.	Common.	Low or dry ground.	Aug.-Sept.	
Gerardia tenuifolia (see Gerardia, Slender).						
Geum rivale (see Avens).						
Gilia tricolor.	Polemonium.	Lilac-purple.	From California, gardens.	Light soil.	July-Sept.	2
Gill-over-the-Ground (see Ground Ivy).						
*Ginseng, A.	Ginseng.	White.	Vt., W. Conn. to Minn., S. to mts. Ga.	Rich, cool woods.	July.	
Gladiolus Blandus.	Iris.	White and pale tints.	Gardens.	Light soil.	Aug., Sept.	197
Gladiolus, Brenchleyensis.						197
Gladiolus, Butterfly.						197

272 FAMILIAR FLOWERS OF FIELD AND GARDEN.

SPECIES AND VARIETIES.	Family.	Color.	Locality.	Environment.	Time of bloom.	Pages.
Gladiolus Byzantinus	Iris.	Purple.	From the Levant, gardens.	Light soil.	Aug., Sept.	197
Gladiolus cardinalis	Iris.	Bright scarlet.	From Cape of Good Hope, gardens.	Light soil.	Aug., Sept.	197
Gladiolus, Ceres		Pink and purplish and white.	From S. Europe, gardens.	Light soil.	Aug., Sept.	197
Gladiolus, Chrysolora						197
Gladiolus communis	Iris.					196
Gladiolus Gandavensis						197
Gladiolus, Madame Monneret						197
Gladiolus psittacinus	Iris.	Yellow, red striped.	From Cape of Good Hope, gardens.	Light soil.	Aug., Sept.	196
Glycyrrhiza glabra (see Licorice)						151
Godetia amœna	Evening-Primrose.	White and crimson, magenta-pink.	Cal. and Ore., gardens.	Light soil.	July–Sept.	
Godetia purpurea	Evening-Primrose.	Purple, dark center.	Ore. and Cal., gardens.	Light soil.	July–Sept.	
*Golden Aster (see Chrysopsis).						
*Golden-Club, O	Arum.	Golden-yellow.	Mass. to Fla.	Ponds.	May.	216
Golden Rod (see Solidago)						82
Goldthread, C	Crowfoot.	White.	Common N. S. to Md. in mts., and W. to Iowa.	Bogs, damp, cold woods.	Apr., May.	
Goodyera pubescens (see Rattlesnake-Plantain).						64
Goodyera repens	Orchis.	Greenish white.	Northward and in Alleghanies.	Woods under evergreens.	July.	64
Gossypium herbaceum (see Cotton)						194
Grape-Hyacinth, M	Lily.	Pale ultramarine-blue.	From Europe, escaped from cultivation, gardens.	Copses and fields.	Apr.	200

A SYSTEMATICAL INDEX.

*Grass of Parnassus, P.	Saxifrage.	White, green, or yellow veins.		Wet banks.	Sept.	2
Ground Ivy, N	Mint.	Light violet.	Common.	Waste or cultivated shady grounds.	Apr.–July.	
Ground Nut, A	Ginseng.	White, greenish.	N. E. to Minn., S. to Ga.	Rich woods.	Apr., May.	68, 185
Gnaphalium polycephalum (see Everlasting, Common).						
Habenaria fimbriata (see Orchis, Fringed)						
Habenaria lacera	Orchis.	Pale greenish.	N. E. to N. C. and Ga., W. to Minn. and Mo.	Bogs and moist thickets.	July.	65 67
Habenaria psycodes	Orchis.	Purplish magenta.	N. E. to N. C., W. to Ind. and Minn.	Wet meadows and bogs.	July, Aug.	67
Habenaria virescens	Orchis.	Dull greenish.	N. E. to Fla., W. to Minn. and Mo.	Wet places.	June, July.	67
Hamamelis Virginica (see Witch-Hazel).						188
Hardhack, S	Rose.	Light pink.	N. E. to mts. of Ga., W. to Minn. and Kan.	Roadsides and low grounds.	June–Sept.	169
Harebell (see Bluebell).						165, 237
*Helenium autumnale (see Sneeze-Weed).						
Helianthus angustifolius	Composite.	Brown and golden yellow.	N. J., southward, and to Kan.	Pine barrens.	Aug., Sept.	209
Helianthus annuus (see Sunflower, Garden)						208
Helianthus argophyllus	Composite.	Golden yellow.	From Texas, gardens.	Open ground.	Aug., Sept.	208 208
Helianthus Cucumerifolius (see Sutton's Miniature Sunflower).						
*Helianthus divaricatus	Composite.	All yellow.	Common.	Thickets and barrens.	Aug, Sept.	178, 209
Helianthus giganteus (see Sunflower, Wild).						

274 FAMILIAR FLOWERS OF FIELD AND GARDEN.

Species and Varieties.	Family.	Color.	Locality.	Environment.	Time of bloom.	Pages.
Helianthus heterophyllus.................	Composite.	Brown and golden yellow.	Ga. and southward.	Pine barrens.	Aug., Sept.	209
Helianthus Maximiliani (see Sunflower, Maximilian's).						209
Helianthus occidentalis.................	Composite.	All golden yellow.	Ohio to Wis. Minn. and southward.	Dry barrens.	Aug., Sept.	209
*Helianthus orgyalis..................	Composite.	Brown and yellow.	Mo. to Neb., S. and W., and gardens.	Dry plains.	Aug., Sept.	
Heliotrope, H.......................	Borage.	Violet-purple lilac, white.	From Peru, Chili, gardens.	Light soil.	June-Sept.	106
Heliotropium Peruvianum (see Heliotrope)...						106
Hellebore, False White (see Indian Poke)...						79
*Hemerocallis flava (see Day-Lily, Yellow).						
Hepatica triloba, L...................	Crowfoot.	Pale blue-purple and whitish.	Atlantic States, W. to Mo. and Minn., and northward.	Pastures and woods.	Mar., Apr.	8
Herb Robert, G.......................	Geranium.	Purple-brown crimson.	N. E. to Mo., and northward.	Moist woods and shaded ravines.	June-Oct.	79, 119
*Hesperis matronalis (see Rocket).						
Hibiscus coccineus (see Rose-Mallow, Scarlet).						193
*Hibiscus militaris (see Rose-Mallow, Halberd-leaved).						
Hibiscus Moscheutos (see Rose-Mallow, Swamp).						193
Hibiscus Syriacus (see Althæa, Shrubby)...						194
*Hieracium venosum (see Rattlesnake-Weed).						
Hobble-Bush, V.......................	Honeysuckle.	White.	N. E. to Ont. and Pa. and mts. to N. C.	Cold, moist woods.	May.	80
Holly, American, I....................	Holly.	White.	Me. to N. J. near coast, W. to S. Mo., and southward.	Moist woodlands.	June.	245

A SYSTEMATICAL INDEX. 275

Holly, English, I.		Holly.	White.	Gardens.	Good soil, open ground.	June.	245
Holly, Mountain, N.		Holly.	White.	Mts. of Va. to Me., Ind., Wis., and northward.	Damp, cold woods.	May.	245
Hollyhock, A.		Mallow.	Various.	From Syria, gardens.	Good soil.	Aug., Sept.	192
Honeysuckle, L.		Honeysuckle.	Pink-red and white.	Gardens.	Good soil.	June–Aug.	61, 97
*Horse-Balm, C.		Mint.	Pale yellow.	N. E. to Wis., S. to Fla. and Mo.	Rich, moist woods.	July–Sept.	
*Horse-Nettle, S.		Nightshade.	Pale violet.	Conn. to Iowa, S. to Fla. and Tex.	Sandy soil and waste places.	June–Aug.	
Houstonia cærulea (see Bluets)							
Hudsonia tomentosa		Rock-rose.	Yellow.	Me. to Md., and the Great Lakes to Minn.	Sandy shores.	May, June.	48
Hyacinth, Cultivated, H		Lily.	Various.	From the Levant, gardens.	Light soil.	Apr., May.	200
Hyacinth, Wild (see Wild Hyacinth).							5
Hyacinthus orientalis (see Hyacinth, Cultivated)							200
Hypericum densiflorum (see Shrubby St. John's-wort).							121
Hypericum maculatum.		St. John's-wort.	Pale yellow.	Common.	Damp places.	July–Sept.	121, 123
Hypericum perforatum (see St. John's-wort, Common).							
Hypoxys erecta (see Yellow Star-Grass).							50
Iberis Gibraltica		Mustard.	Crimson-pink and white.	From Europe, gardens.	Light soil.	May, June.	89
Iberis sempervirens.		Mustard.	White.	From Europe, gardens.	Light soil.	May.	89
Iberis umbellata (see Candytuft).							88

276 FAMILIAR FLOWERS OF FIELD AND GARDEN.

SPECIES AND VARIETIES.	Family.	Color.	Locality.	Environment.	Time of bloom.	Pages.
Ilex Aquifolium (see English Holly)						245
Ilex lævigata (see Winterberry, Smooth)						244
Ilex opaca (see American Holly)						245
Ilex verticillata (see Black Alder)						244
Impatiens balsamina (see Balsam)						116
Impatiens fulva	Geranium.	Orange-spotted brown.	Common, southward.	Wet ground, moist and shady places.	June-Sept.	171
Impatiens pallida (see Jewel-Weed)						171
Indian Cress (see Nasturtium)						111
Indian Cucumber-Root, M.	Lily.	Pale green-ish-yellow.	N.E. to Minn., Ind., and southward.	Rich, damp woods.	June.	109
Indian Pipe, M.	Heath.	Pinkish white.	Common.	Rich woods.	June-Aug.	98
Indian Poke, V.	Lily.	Yellowish green.	Common.	Swamps and low grounds.	June-Aug.	79
*Indian Shot (see Canna Indica).						
Indian Tobacco, L.	Lobelia.	Light blue-violet, pale-blue and white.	Common.	Dry, open fields.	June-Aug.	176
Indian Turnip (see Jack-in-the-Pulpit)						6, 23, 42
*Indigofera tinctoria (see Indigo Plant).						
*Indigo-Plant, I.						
*Indigo, Wild, B.	Pulse.	Yellow.	Particularly South, common.	Waste places.	July, Aug.	
*Inula Helenium (see Elecampane).	Pulse.	Yellow.	N. E. to Fla., W. to Minn. and La.	Sandy, dry soil.	May, June.	
Ipomœa purpurea (see Morning-Glory).						
*Iris Florentina.						135
*Iris fulva	Iris.	Copper, or red-brown.	South Ill. and Mo. to La. and Ga.	Swamps.	May.	107
Iris Kæmpferi.	Iris.	Various.	From Japan, gardens.	Moist ground.	June, July.	74

A SYSTEMATICAL INDEX.

Iris prismatica or Virginica	Iris.	Violet-blue.	Me. to N. C.	Marshes near the coast.	June.	74
Iris versicolor (see Flag, Larger Blue)						73
Iron-weed, V	Composite.	Crimson-magenta.	Me. to Va., W. to Minn., Kan., and southward.	Low grounds near the coast.	Aug., Sept.	90, 234
Ivy, Poison (see Poison Ivy)						137
Jack-in-the-Pulpit, A	Arum.	Green and purple-brown.	N. E. to Fla., W. to Minn. and E. Kan.	Rich woods.	May.	6, 14, 42, 74
*Jasminum officinale (see Jessamine, White). Jerusalem Cherry, S	Night-shade.	White.	From Madeira, conservatories and gardens.	Light, rich soil.	June, July.	244
*Jessamine, White, J	Olive.	White.	From Orient, conservatories and gardens.	Rich soil.	Apr.–June.	
*Jessamine, Yellow (false), G	Logania.	Yellow.	East Va. to Fla. and Tex.	Low grounds.	Mar., Apr.	
Jewel-Weed, I	Geranium.	Spotted brown-orange and yellow.	Common, northward.	Moist, shady ground and along rills.	July–Sept.	116, 119, 171
Joe-Pye Weed, E	Composite.	Flesh-color.	Common.	Low grounds.	Aug., Sept.	212
Jonquil, N	Amaryllis.	Golden yellow.	Gardens.	Damp, good soil.	Apr., May.	108
Kalmia angustifolia (see Sheep Laurel)						87
Kalmia glauca	Heath.	Purple-lilac.	Newf. to Pa., Minn. and northward.	Cold peat bogs and mts.	May, June.	87

278 FAMILIAR FLOWERS OF FIELD AND GARDEN.

SPECIES AND VARIETIES.	Family.	Color.	Locality.	Environment.	Time of bloom.	Pages.
Kalmia latifolia, M..............	Heath.	Pinkish and white.	Canada and Me. mts. to W. Fla. W. to O., Ky., and Tenn.	Rocky hills and damp soil.	June.	85
Kniphofia aloides (see Tritoma)..						
*Knotweed, Common, P............	Buck-wheat.	White and flesh-color.	Common.	Yards and waste places.	Aug., Sept.	199
*Knotweed, Pink, P................	Buck-wheat.	Magenta-pink.	Common.	Moist soil, waste places.	Aug., Sept.	
*Krigia amplexicaulis.............	Composite.	Light golden yellow.	Conn. to Minn. and southward.	Moist banks.	June.	
Krigia Dandelion (see Cynthia Dandelion).						104, 242
*Krigia Virginica, D..............	Composite.	Light golden yellow.	N. E. to Minn. and southward.	Open grounds.	Apr.-Aug.	
*Labrador Tea, L..................	Heath.	White.	N. E. to Pa., Mich., Minn., and northward.	Cold bogs and mountain woods.	June, July.	
Ladies' Tresses (see Spiranthes cernua).....						214
Lady's Slipper, Larger Yellow (see Cypripedium pubescens).						58
Lady's Slipper, Pink (see Moccason Flower)..						56
Lady's Slipper (see Balsam)...............						116, 119
Lady's Slipper, Smaller Yellow, C............	Orchis.	Bright yellow.	N. E. to Ga., W. to Minn. and E. Kan.	Bogs and low woods.	May, June.	58
Larkspur, Bee, D...................	Crowfoot.	Various.	From Europe, gardens.	Light soil.	July-Sept.	190
Larkspur, Rocket, D...............	Crowfoot.	Various.	Gardens.	Light soil.	July-Sept.	191
Lathyrus odoratus (see Sweet Pea).........						114, 204
Laurel, Great (see *Rhododendron maximum*)..						61
Laurel, Mountain (see *Kalmia latifolia*).....						85

A SYSTEMATICAL INDEX.

Name	Family	Color	Range	Habitat	Time	Page
Laurel, Sheep (see Sheep Laurel).						87
*Ledum latifolium (see Labrador Tea).						
Lemon Verbena						23
Leontodon autumnalis (see Fall Dandelion).						104, 241
*Lespedeza procumbens (see Bush-Clover).						
Liatris scariosa (see Blazing-Star).						90, 194
*Liatris squarrosa	Composite.	Magenta-purple.	Pa. to Minn. and southward.	Dry soil.	Aug., Sept.	151
Licorice, G.						236
Lilac, White.						125
Lilium Canadense (see Lily, Yellow Field).						125
Lilium Philadelphicum (see Lily, Wild Red Wood).						126
Lilium superbum (see Lily, Turk's-Cap).						126
Lilium tigrinum (see Lily, Tiger).						67, 160
Lily-of-the-Valley, C.	Lily.	White.	From Europe, gardens.	Partially shady, rich soil.	May, June.	
Lily, Tiger, L.	Lily.	Brown-spotted, scarlet-red.	From E. Asia, gardens, and near them.	Rich soil.	July, Aug.	126
Lily, Turk's-Cap, L.	Lily.	Orange, brown-spotted.	N. E. to Ga., W. to Minn. and Mo.	Rich low grounds.	June, July.	126
Lily, White Water, N (see Water Lily).						185
Lily, Wild Red Wood, L.	Lily.	Brown-spotted, red-orange and scarlet-red.	N. E. to N. C., W. to Minn. and Mo.	Open woods, dry soil.	June, July.	126
Lily, Yellow Field, L.	Lily.	Golden-yellow and orange-yellow, brown-spotted.	N. E. to Ga., W. to Minn. and Mo.	Moist meadows and bogs.	June, July.	125, 158
Liverwort or Liver-leaf (see *Hepatica*).						8
Linaria Canadensis (see Toadflax, Blue).						174
Linaria vulgaris (see Toadflax, Yellow).						173

280 FAMILIAR FLOWERS OF FIELD AND GARDEN.

SPECIES AND VARIETIES.	Family.	Color.	Locality.	Environment.	Time of bloom.	Pages.
*Linnæa borealis (see Twin-Flower).						177
*Linum grandiflorum (see Flax, Crimson).						176
Lobelia cardinalis (see Cardinal-Flower).						176
Lobelia erinus.	Lobelia.	Violet.	Cape of Good Hope, gardens.	Rich soil.	July–Sept.	176
Lobelia inflata (see Indian Tobacco).						176
Lobelia Kalmii.	Lobelia.	Light violet.	N. E. to Minn., S. to Pa. and Ind.	Wet banks.	July–Sept.	176
Lobelia syphilitica.	Lobelia.	Light blue-violet.	Common.	Low grounds.	July–Sept.	176
Lonicera Japonica (see Honeysuckle).						61, 97
Loosestrife, Common, L.	Primrose.	Yellow.	N. E. to Minn., Ark., and N. Ga.	Low grounds.	June–Aug.	156
Loosestrife, Four-leaved, L.	Primrose.	Yellow.	N. E. to Minn. and Ga.	Moist or sandy soil.	June, July.	155
Loosestrife, Purple, L.	Loose-strife.	Pale magenta-purple.	N. E. to Del.	Wet meadows.	June–Aug.	156
Love-in-a-Mist, N.	Crowfoot.	Bluish white.	From Orient, gardens.	Light soil.	July–Sept.	154
Love-lies-Bleeding, A.	Amaranth.	Pale dull crimson.	From China, gardens.	Light soil.	Aug, Sept.	121
*Lychnis Githago (see Corn-Cockle).						195
Lycopsis arvensis (see Bugloss, Small).						155
Lysimachia quadrifolia (see Loosestrife, Four-leaved).						
Lysimachia stricta (see Loosestrife, Common).						156
Lythrum Salicaria (see Loosestrife, Purple).						156
Maianthemum Canadense, S.	Lily.	White.	N. E. to N. C., W. to Minn. and Iowa.	Moist woods and banks.	May.	40
Mallow, Common, M.	Mallow.	White.	Common.	Fields and roadsides.	June–Oct.	192

A SYSTEMATICAL INDEX. 281

Mallow, Musk, M	Mallow.	Pale magenta-pink.	From Europe, escaped from cultivation, gardens.	Roadsides.	July–Sept.	192
Malva moschata (see Musk Mallow).						192
Malva rotundifolia (see Mallow, Common).						192
Marigold, African, T	Composite.	Yellow and orange.	From Mexico and S. America, gardens.	Light soil.	Aug., Sept.	202, 203, 206
						203
Marigold, El Dorado						203
Marigold, French, T	Composite.	Golden yellow, maroon and orange.	From Mexico and S. America, gardens.	Light soil.	July–Sept.	
						147
Marigold, Garden (see Calendula)						203
Marigold, Legion d'Honneur						192
Marsh Mallow, A	Mallow.	Pinkish.	Coast of N. E. and N. Y.	Salt marshes.	Aug., Sept.	
Marsh Marigold, C	Crowfoot.	Golden yellow.	Common northward.	Swamps and wet meadows.	Apr., May.	6
*Marsh Rosemary (see Sea Lavender).						
*Marsh St. John's-wort (see St. John's-wort, Marsh).						
*Marvel-of-Peru (see Four-o'clock).						
*May-apple, P	Barberry.	White.	Common,	Rich woods.	May.	1
Mayflower (see Arbutus).						
*Meadow Beauty, R	Melastoma.	Magenta-pink.	Common northward.	Sandy swamps.	June–Aug.	
Meadow-rue, Early, T	Crowfoot.	Greenish and purplish.	Common.	Rocky woods and pastures.	Apr., May.	159
Meadow-rue, Tall, T	Crowfoot.	White.	N. E. to Ohio and southward, common.	Roadsides, wet meadows.	July–Sept.	18, 158
Meadow-Sweet, S	Rose.	White or flesh-color.	N. E. to mts. Ga. W. to Minn. and Mo.	Wet or low grounds.	May, June.	168
Medeola Virginica (see Indian Cucumber-Root).						109

SPECIES AND VARIETIES.	Family.	Color.	Locality.	Environment.	Time of bloom.	Pages.
Melilotus officinalis (see Melilot).						
*Melilot, Yellow, M	Pulse.	Yellow.	Common.	Waste or cultivated grounds.	June–Aug.	137
Mercury Vine (see Poison Ivy).						198
Mexican Star Flower (see *Milla biflora*).						91
Mignonette, R.	Mignon-ette.	Greenish, yellowish, and whitish.	From the Levant, gardens.	Sandy soil.	June–Sept.	
Milkweed, Common, A	Milkweed.	Dull lilac-brown and brown-lilac.	Common.	Rich soil and beside copses.	June–Aug.	162
Milkwort (see *Polygala sanguinea*, etc).						108, 109
Milla biflora, M	Lily.	White.	From Mexico, gardens.	Light soil.	July, Aug.	198, 202
Mirabilis Jalapa (see Four-o'clock).						
Mitchella repens (see Partridge-berry).						82
Mitella diphylla, M.	Saxifrage.	White.	N.E. to N.C.,W. to Minn and Mo.	Rich grounds of hillsides.	May.	26
Mitella nuda	Saxifrage.	Greenish white.	N.E. to N.Y., Mich., Minn., and northward.	Deep moist woods in moss.	May–July.	26
Mitrewort, False (see *Tiarella cordifolia*).						25
Mitrewort, True (see *Mitella diphylla*).						26
Moccason Flower, Pink, C	Orchis.	Crimson-pink.	N.E. to N.C.,W. to N. Ind., Mich., and Minn.	Woods.	May, June.	56, 214
Molucca Balm, M	Mint.	Green.	From Molucca Islands, gardens.	Good soil, somewhat sandy.	July–Sept.	189
Moluccella laevis (see Molucca Balm).						189
Monarda didyma (see Oswego Tea).						

A SYSTEMATICAL INDEX.

Monkshood (see Aconite)					
Monotropa Hypopitys (see False Beech-drops)					
Monotropa uniflora (see Indian Pipe)					
Morning-Glory, I	Convolvulus.	Various.	From trop. America, gardens.	Light soil.	July–Oct.	191, 196 100 98 73, 135
Moss Pink, P	Polemonium.	Crimson-pink.	Cultivated, and S. N. Y. to Mich., S. to Fla. and Ky.	Rocky hills, sandy banks.	May, June.	53
Mountain Daisy (see Sandwort)						97
Mountain Holly (see Holly, Mountain)						245
Mountain Laurel (see Kalmia latifolia)						85
Mountain Sandwort (see Sandwort)						97
Mourning Bride, S	Teasel.	Various.	From Europe, gardens.	Light, good soil.	July–Oct.	112, 194, 204, 206
Mullein, V	Figwort.	Light yellow.	Common.	Fields and pastures.	July–Sept.	182
Muscari botryoides (see Grape-Hyacinth)						200
Mustard, Wild Black, B. S	Mustard.	Yellow.	Common.	Fields and waste places.	June–Sept.	83
Myosotis palustris (see Forget-me-not)						90
Narcissus Jonquilla (see Jonquil)	Amaryllis.	Red-edged cup, white.	Gardens.	Damp, good soil.	Apr., May.	108
Narcissus poeticus						108
Narcissus polyanthos	Amaryllis.	White.	From Europe, gardens.	Partly shady, damp soil.	Apr., May.	108
Narcissus Pseudo-Narcissus (see Daffodil)						108
Narcissus Tazetta (see Narcissus, Polyanthus)						108
Narcissus, Polyanthus, N	Amaryllis.	Yellow and white.	From Europe, gardens.	Damp, good soil.	Apr., May.	108
Nasturtium, T	Geranium.	Various.	From Peru and Chili, gardens.	Sandy soil.	June–Sept.	111, 119, 150
Nasturtium, Asa Gray						112
Nasturtium, Aurora						112
Nasturtium, Crystal Palace Gem						112
Nasturtium, Edward Otto						112
Nasturtium, Empress of India						112

284 FAMILIAR FLOWERS OF FIELD AND GARDEN.

SPECIES AND VARIETIES.	Family.	Color.	Locality.	Environment.	Time of bloom.	Pages.
Nasturtium, King of Tom Thumbs						112
Nasturtium, King Theodore						112
Nasturtium, Pearl						112
Nasturtium, Prince Henry						112
Nasturtium, Rose						112
Nasturtium officinale (see Water-Cress)						115
Nemopanthes, Canadensis or *fascicularis* (see Holly, Mountain).						245
Nepeta Glechoma (see Ground Ivy)						2
*New Jersey Tea, C.	Buckthorn.	White.	Common.	Dry woodlands.	July.	76, 101,
Nicotiana affinis (see Tobacco, White-flowered)						190
Nicotiana Tabacum (see Tobacco, Common)						190
Nigella Damascena (see Love-in-a-Mist)						154, 191
Nightshade (Bittersweet), S.	Night-shade.	Violet-purple.	From Europe, common.	Waste and moist ground.	June-Aug.	242
*Nightshade, Common, S.	Night-shade.	White.	Common.	Shaded grounds and fields.	July-Sept.	
Nuphar advena (see Pond-Lily, Yellow).						185
Nymphæa odorata (see White Water-Lily).						
Oakesia sessilifolia (see Bellwort).						15
Œnothera amœna (see Godetia amœna).						
Œnothera biennis (see Evening-Primrose).						
*Œnothera fruticosa	Evening-Primrose.	Light yellow.	Common.	Open places.	June, July.	76
*Œnothera Missouriensis	Evening-Primrose.	Yellow.	Mo. and Kan. to Tex.	Open places.	June-Aug.	
Œnothera pumila (see Sundrops)						76
Œnothera purpurea (see Godetia purpurea).						
Old-Man's-Beard (see *Clematis Virginiana*)						138

A SYSTEMATICAL INDEX.

Opuntia vulgaris (see Prickly-Pear).						
Orchis, Fringed, H..............	Orchis.	Purplish pink-magenta.	N. E. to N. J. and N. C., W. to Mich.	Wet meadows.	June.	65
Orchis, Showy, O...............	Orchis.	Pink-purple and white.	N.E. to Ga., W. to Minn. and Mo.	Rich woods.	May, June.	67
Orchis spectabilis (see Showy Orchis)...						67
Ornithogalum umbellatum (see Star of Bethlehem).						101
Orontium aquaticum (see Golden-Club).						
Osmorrhiza brevistylis................	Parsley.	White.	From N. E. westward, and mts. to N. C.	Rich, moist woods.	May, June.	
Osmorrhiza longistylis (see Sweet Cicely).						
*Oswego Tea, M	Mint.	Red.	N. E., W. and S., cultivated.	Dry soil.	July, Aug.	71 71
Oxalis Acetosella (see Wood-Sorrel, White).						
Oxalis stricta (see Wood-Sorrel, Yellow).						
Oxalis violacea (see Woo(.-Sorrel, Violet).						
Ox-eye Daisy (see Daisy, Ox-eye)........						105
Pæonia officinalis (see Pæony).						
*Pæony, P...............	Crowfoot.	Various.	From Europe, gardens.	Good soil.	May.	
*Painted-Cup. C................	Figwort.	Pale yellow and purplish.	Me. to Minn. S. to N. J., Tenn, and Tex.	Low, sandy grounds.	June.	
Pansy, V....................	Violet.	Various.	From Europe, gardens.	Rich, cool ground.	Apr.-Aug.	10
Pansy, Bugnot.................						11
Pansy, Cassier's Odier.........						11
Papaver dubium						141
Papaver glaucium (see Tulip P.)						142
Papaver nudicaude (see Iceland P.)						142
Papaver Orientale (see Oriental P.)						142
Papaver Rhœas (see Corn P.)						142

SPECIES AND VARIETIES.	Family.	Color.	Locality.	Environment.	Time of bloom.	Pages.
Papaver somniferum (see Opium P.)						142
*Parnassia Caroliniana (see Grass of Parnassus)						96
Parsnip, Common Wild, P.						96
Parsnip, Wild Meadow, Z.	Parsley.	Yellow.	Common.	Meadows, fields.	Aug.	96
Partridge-Berry, M.	Parsley.	Yellow.	Atlantic States, W. to Minn. and Tex.	Fields and roadsides.	May, June.	96
	Madder.	White, pink-tipped.	Common East and South.	Woods, dry and wet places.	June, July.	82
*Pasque-Flower, Wild (see Anemone patens).						
Pastinaca sativa (see Parsnip, Common Wild).						96
*Pedicularis Canadensis (see Wood Betony).						
Pelargonium (see Geranium, Flowering).						
Pelargonium angulosum (see P., Maple-leaved).						116
Pelargonium capitatum (see Rose-scented P.).						200
Pelargonium cordatum (see P., Heart-leaved).						117
Pelargonium cucullatum (see P., Cowled).						200
Pelargonium erstipulatum (see Penny-royal P.)						200
Pelargonium inquinans (see Scarlet P.).						117
Pelargonium peltatum (see Ivy-leaved P.).						118
Pelargonium Radula (see Scented or Rough P.)						118
Pelargonium tomentosum (see Peppermint P.).						119
Pelargonium Zonale (see Horseshoe P.).						118
Pelargonium, Cowled						117
Pelargonium, Heart-leaved						118
Pelargonium, Horseshoe						200
Pelargonium, Ivy-leaved						200
Pelargonium, Maple-leaved						118
Pelargonium, Penny-royal						118
Pelargonium, Peppermint						200
Pelargonium, Rose-scented						117
Pelargonium, Scarlet						117
Pelargonium, Scented or Rough						118
*Periwinkle, V.	Dogbane.	Violet.	From Europe, gardens.	Partially shady, light soil.	Apr., May.	119

A SYSTEMATICAL INDEX.

Petunia nyctaginiflora	Night-shade.	White.	From S. America, gardens.	Light soil.	July–Sept.	188
Petunia violacea	Night-shade.	Magenta and purple.	From S. America, gardens.	Light soil.	July–Sept.	188
Petunia, Defiance						189
Petunia, Giants of California						188
Petunia, Green Margin						189
Petunia, Kermesina splendens						189
*Phacelia Whitlavia (see Whitlavia grandiflora)						
Phlox decussata	Polemonium.	Various.	Hybrid var., gardens.	Light soil.	June–Aug.	92, 93
Phlox divaricata	Polemonium.	Lilac, blue-lilac.	N. Y. to Minn., S. to Fla. and Ark.	Rocky, damp woods.	May.	93
Phlox Drummondii	Polemonium.	Various.	From Texas, gardens.	Light soil.	June–Oct.	92
Phlox Drummondii cuspidata (see Star of Quedlinburg).						92
Phlox Drummondii fimbriata		Pink or whitish.		Prairies and open woods.	June, July.	92
Phlox glaberrima	Polemonium.		N. Va. to Ohio and Minn., S. to Fla. and Mo.			94
Phlox maculata	Polemonium.	Pale magenta and white.	N. J. and N. Pa. to Minn., S. to Fla. and Ark.	Rich woodlands and along streams.	June–Aug.	93
Phlox ovata or Carolina	Polemonium.	Pink, deep pink.	Mts. from Pa. to Ala.	Open woods.	June, July.	94
Phlox, Star of Quedlinburg, P						93
Phlox subulata (see Moss Pink)						53, 94
Phytolacca decandra (see Garget).						236
Pigweed, Common, A	Amaranth.	Green.		Cultivated grounds.	July, Aug.	121
Pincushion Flower (see Mourning Bride)						208
Pinxter Flower (see Purple or Pink Azalea)						60
Pipsissewa, C	Heath.	Flesh-color.	N. E. to Ga., W. to the Pacific.	Dry, sandy soil, woods.	June, July.	70

288 FAMILIAR FLOWERS OF FIELD AND GARDEN.

SPECIES AND VARIETIES.	Family.	Color.	Locality.	Environment.	Time of bloom.	Pages.
Pitcher-Plant, S.	Pitcher-plant.	Deep ruddy purple.	N. E. to Minn., N. Iowa, and S.E. of Alleghanies.	Peat bogs.	May, June.	45
*Podophyllum peltatum (see May-Apple).						
Pogonia ophioglossoides (see Snake's Mouth).						
Poinsettia (of Mexico), E.	Spurge.	The tip leaves scarlet.	From Mexico, conservatories and gardens.	Rich soil.	Winter.	59, 202, 210
*Poinsettia (of the United States), E.	Spurge.	The tip leaves scarlet.	Minn. to W. Ill., Iowa and Miss., and gardens.	Slopes and rocky soil.	Aug.	
Poison Ivy, R.	Cashew.	Greenish or yellowish white.	Common.	Thickets, low grounds.	June.	137
Poke or Pigeon Berry (see Garget).						
Polianthes tuberosa (see Tuberose).						236
*Polygala fastigiata	Polygala or milkwort.	Pink-purple, crimson.	Pines of N. J., Del., Ky., southward.	Sandy soil.	June-Aug.	107, 202
Polygala lutea.	Polygala or milkwort.	Orange-yellow.	From N. J. southward.	Sandy swamps, near coast.	June-Aug.	109
Polygala paucifolia, F.	Polygala or milkwort.	Pink-purple.	N. E. to Minn. and Ill. S. in Alleghanies.	Woods, light soil.	May.	30
Polygala sanguinea, M.	Polygala or milkwort.	Pink or purplish crimson.	Common.	Sandy and moist ground.	June-Aug.	108
Polygala senega.	Polygala or milkwort.	White.	W. N. E. to Minn. and southward.	Rocky soil.	May, June.	109
Polygala polygama.	Polygala or milkwort.	Pink-purple.	Common.	Dry, sandy soil.	July.	109
Polygonatum biflorum (see Solomon's Seal).						36

A SYSTEMATICAL INDEX. 289

	Water-lily.	Yellow.	Common.	Still or stagnant water.	June–Aug.	
Polygonum arifolium (see Tear Thumb).						
Polygonum aviculare (see Knotweed, Common)						
Polygonum Pennsylvanicum (see Knotweed, Pink).						
Polygonum scandens (see Buckwheat, Climbing False).						
*Pond-Lily, Yellow, N.	Water-lily.					144, 145
Poppy, Bride						142
Poppy, California (see *Eschscholtzia Californica*)						148
Poppy, California Tree, D						142, 143,
Poppy, Carnation Flower						147, 204
						142
Poppy, Corn						144
Poppy, Eider Down						13, 143
Poppy, Fairy Blush						147
Poppy, Flag-of-Truce						142, 145
Poppy, Iceland						143
Poppy, Mikado						144
Poppy, New Cardinal						142, 147
Poppy, Opium						142, 145
Poppy, Oriental						142, 143,
Poppy, Peony Flower						147
						142, 143,
Poppy, Ranunculus Flower						147
						143
Poppy, Rosy Morn						143, 146
Poppy, Shirley						145
Poppy, Snowdrift						142
Poppy, Tulip						146
Poppy, Umbrosum						77, 120
Portulaca, P	Purslane.	Various.	Gardens.	Sandy, sunny grounds.	June–Sept.	120, 152
Portulaca grandiflora (see Portulaca)						120
Portulaca oleracea (see Purslane)						50
Potentilla Canadensis (see Cinquefoil, Common)						52
Potentilla fruticosa (see Cinquefoil, Shrubby)						51
Potentilla Norvegica (see Cinquefoil, Norway)						7, 149
Pot Marigold (see *Calendula officinalis*)						

SPECIES AND VARIETIES.	Family.	Color.	Locality.	Environment.	Time of bloom.	Pages.
*Prickly Pear, O.	Cactus.	Pale yellow.	Nantucket to S. C., near coast.	Sandy fields and dry rocks.	July-Sept.	149
Prickly Poppy, White (see *Argemone, var. albiflora*).						
Prickly Poppy, Yellow, A.	Poppy.	Yellow.	Waste places, southward, and gardens.	Light soil.	July-Sept.	142, 146
Prince's Feather, A.	Amaranth.	Deep crimson.	From India, gardens.	Light soil.	Aug., Sept.	121
Purple-flowering Raspberry, R.	Rose.	Magenta-crimson, pink.	N. E. to N. J. and Ga., W. to Mich.	Hedges and roadsides.	June, July.	123
Purslane or Pusley, P.	Purslane.	Pale yellow.	Common weed, gardens.	Common soil.	June-Aug.	120
Pyrethrum or Feverfew (see *Chrysanthemum Parthenium*).						105
Pyrethrum roseum (see *Chrysanthemum roseum*)						105
Pyrola elliptica (see Shin-Leaf).						69
Ragwort (see Golden Senecio)						68
Ranunculus fascicularis (see Buttercup, Early)						103
Ranunculus poppy (see Poppy Ranunculus).						142
Ranunculus repens (see Buttercup, Common).						102
Raspberry, Purple-Flowering (see Purple Flowering Raspberry).						123
*Rattlebox, C.	Pulse.	Yellow.	Me. to Ill., Minn., Kan. and southward.	Sandy soil.	June-Aug.	
Rattlesnake-Plantain, G.	Orchis.	Greenish white.	N. E. to Fla. W. to Mich. and Minn.	Rich woods.	July.	64, 215
*Rattlesnake-Weed, H.	Composite.	Golden yellow.	Atlantic States to Minn. and Iowa.	Pine woods, plains.	July-Sept.	

Red-hot-poker Plant (see Tritoma Uvaria)					199
Reseda glauca					92
Reseda luteola	Mignonette.	Dull yellowish.	N. Y. and rarely in N. E.	Roadsides and waysides.	Aug.	91
Reseda odorata (see Mignonette)						91
Reseda sesamoides						92
*Rhexia Virginica (see Meadow Beauty)						
Rhododendron arboreum						63
*Rhododendron calendulaceum (see Azalea calendulacea)						
Rhododendron Catawbiense	Heath.	Lilac-purple.	High Alleghanies, Va. to Ga.	Deep and open woods.	June.	63
Rhododendron maximum, L	Heath.	Nearly white and pink.	Rare Me. to Ohio, common Alleghanies from N. Y. to Ga.	Damp, deep woods.	June, July.	61
Rhododendron nudiflorum (see Azalea nudiflora)						61
Rhododendron Ponticum						63
Rhododendron Rhodora (see Rhodora Canadensis)						61
*Rhododendron viscosum (see Azalea viscosa)						
Rhodora Canadensis, R	Heath.	Magenta-pink.	N. E. to mts. of Pa.	Cool bogs.	May, June.	61
Rhus Toxicodendron (see Poison Ivy)						137
Richardia Africana (see Calla Æthiopian)						6, 14, 132
Ricinus communis (see Castor-oil Plant)						222
Robin's Plantain, E	Composite.	Light violet.	Common.	Copses and moist banks.	May, June.	47
*Rocket, H	Mustard.	Purple.	Sparingly naturalized, from Europe, and gardens.	Rich, shady ground.	July-Sept.	
Rose						120, 123, 124, 147
*Rose-Mallow, Halberd-leaved, H	Mallow.	Flesh-color, purple base.	Pa. to Minn. and southward.	River banks.	Aug. Sept.	

SPECIES AND VARIETIES.	Family.	Color.	Locality.	Environment.	Time of bloom.	Pages.
Rose-Mallow, Scarlet, H.	Mallow.	Red-scarlet.	Carolina and southward.	Swamps.	Aug., Sept.	193
Rose-Mallow, Swamp, H.	Mallow.	Pale pink.	E. Mass. and southward, W., to Ill. and Mo.	Marshes and swamps.	Aug., Sept.	193
Rose of Sharon (see Althæa, Shrubby).						
*Rosin-Weed, S.	Composite.	Yellow.		Prairies.	July.	194
Rubus odoratus (see Purple-Flowering Raspberry).						
Rudbeckia hirta, B.	Composite.	Deep golden yellow.	Mich., Dak., and southward.			123
*Rudbeckia laciniata.	Composite.	Deep yellow.	W. N. Y. to Wis. and southward, meadows eastward.	Dry soil and sandy ground.	June, July.	127, 208
*Rudbeckia speciosa.	Composite.	Deep yellow.	Common.	Low thickets.	July–Sept.	
Rue Anemone (see Anemone, Rue).			W. Pa. to Mich., Mo. and southward.	Dry soil.	July.	
Rumex Acetosella (see Sheep Sorrel).						17, 34 72
*Sabbatia angularis.	Gentian.	Light pink.	N. Y. to Ont. and Mich., S. to Fla.	Rich soil.	June–Aug.	
Sabbatia chloroides	Gentian.	Deep pink.	Mass. to Fla. and Ala.	Borders of brackish ponds.	June–Aug.	
*Sabbatia paniculata	Gentian.	White.	Va. to Fla.	Low grounds.	June–Aug.	75
*Sage, Common, S.	Mint.	Pale blue-violet.	From Europe, gardens.	Light rich soil.	Aug., Sept.	

A SYSTEMATICAL INDEX.

*Sage, Scarlet, S.	Mint.	Scarlet.	From Brazil, gardens.	Light rich soil.	Sept.	75
*Sagittaria variabilis (see Arrow-head).						
*St. Andrew's Cross, A.	St. John's-wort.	Pale yellow.	Nantucket, N. J. to S. Ill., Neb., and southward.	Pine barrens.	July, Aug.	
St. John's-wort, Common, H	St. John's-wort.	Deep yellow.	Common.	Fields and roadsides.	June–Sept.	121
*St. John's-wort, Marsh, E	St. John's-wort.	Flesh-colored.	Common.	In swamps.	July, Aug.	
St. John's-wort, Shrubby, H	St. John's-wort.	Yellow.	N. J. to glades of Ky., Ark., and southward.	Pine barrens, sandy soil.	June, July.	121
*Salpiglossis sinuata, V	Figwort.	Reddish and purplish colors.	From Chili, gardens.	Light soil.	July–Sept.	
*Salvia officinalis (see Sage, Common).						
*Salvia splendens (see Scarlet Sage).						
Sandwort, Mountain, A.	Pink.	White.	N. E. coast, White Mts., Adirondacks, and stony mt. summits.	Between Rocks.	June–Aug.	97, 131
Sanguinaria Canadensis (see Blood-root).						12, 142
Saponaria officinalis (see Bouncing Bet).						187
Sarracenia purpurea (see Pitcher-Plant).						45
Sarsaparilla, True.	Ginseng.	White.	N. E. to Dak., S. to mts. N. C.		May, June.	151
Sarsaparilla, Wild, A.				Moist woodlands.		133
Sassafras officinale	Laurel.	Greenish-yellow.	E. Mass. to Mich., E. Iowa, Kan., and S.	Rich woods.	Apr.	133
Saxifraga Virginiensis (see Saxifrage, Early).						19
Saxifrage, Early, S.	Saxifrage.	White.	N. E. to Ga., W. to Minn. and Tenn.	Dry hillsides.	Apr.–June.	19
Scabiosa atropurpurea (see Mourning Bride).						206
Scilla amœna or Siberica, S.	Lily.	Violet-blue.	From Europe, gardens.	Grassy ground.	Apr., May.	4

SPECIES AND VARIETIES.	Family.	Color.	Locality.	Environment.	Time of bloom.	Pages.
Scilla Frazeri (see Hyacinth, Wild).....	.....	.....	.....	.....	.....	5
Scilla maritima, S.....	Lily.	Pale violet.	Mediterranean region.	Light soil.	Apr., May.	5
Scutellaria lateriflora (see Skullcap).						
*Sea-Lavender, L.....	Leadwort.	Pale dull lilac.	N. E. to Tex., along coast.	Salt marshes.	Aug., Sept.	167 109
Self-heal (see *Brunella vulgaris*).....						
Seneca Snakeroot or Senega (see *Polygala Senega*).						
Senecio aureus (see Golden Senecio).....						
Senecio. Golden, S.....	Composite.	Golden-yellow.	Common.	Open grounds.	May, June.	68
*Senna, Wild, C.....	Pulse.	Yellow.	N. E. to Fla. W. to Mich., S. to Neb., Kan. and La.	Alluvial soil.	June-Aug.	68
Sheep Laurel, K.....	Heath.	Crimson-pink-white.	Common N. E. to Mich., S. to N. Ga.	Low grounds and hilly country	May, June.	87
Sheep Sorrel, R.....	Buckwheat.	Ruddy and green.	From Europe, common.	Sterile ground, fields, etc.	May, June.	72
Shepherd's Purse, C.....	Mustard.	White.	Common.	Waste places and roadsides.	Apr.-Sept.	88, 90
Shin-leaf, P.....	Heath.	Greenish-white.	N. E. to Md., Iowa, Minn. and northward.	Rich woods.	June, July.	69
*Shooting Star (see American Cowslip).						
Shrubby Cinquefoil (see Cinquefoil, Shrubby).						
Silene antirrhina.....	Pink.	Pink.	Common.	Waste places, dry soil.	June-Sept.	51
Silene inflata (see Campion, Bladder).....	.....	.....	.....	.....	.....	120

A SYSTEMATICAL INDEX.

Silene notiflora, C.		Pink.		Common.	June, July.	128
*Silene Pennsylvanica		Pink.	East N. E. to N. Y., Ky., and southward.	Gravelly soil.	Apr.-June.	
Silene stellata (see Campion, Starry).						129
*Silene Virginica		Pink.	West N. Y. to Minn., and southward.	Open woods.	June-Aug.	
Deep red-crimson.						
*Silphium laciniatum (see Rosin-Weed).						132
Simpler's Joy (see Vervain).						83
Sinapis nigra (see Mustard).						49
Sisyrinchium, angustifolium or Bermudiana (see Blue-eyed Grass).						
*Skullcap, Mad-dog, S.	Mint.	Purple-violet.	Common.	Shady places.	June-Aug.	5
Skunk Cabbage, S.	Arum.	Madder-purple and light dull green.	N. E. to N. C., W. to Minn. and Iowa.	Bogs and moist grounds.	Mar., Apr.	
Smilacina bifolia (see Maianthemum Canadense):						40
Smilacina racemosa (see False Solomon's Seal).						37
Smilacina stellata.	Lily.	White.	N. E. to N. J., W. to E. Kan. Minn., and westward.	Moist banks.	May.	39
Smilacina trifolia.	Lily.	White.	N. E. W. to Mich. and Minn.	Cold bogs.	June, July.	40
Snake's Mouth, P.	Orchis.	Pink.	N. E. to Fla., W. to N. Ind. and Minn.	Bogs.	June, July.	59
Snapdragon, Large, A.	Figwort.	Various.	From Europe, gardens.	Good soil.	July-Sept.	157, 174
*Sneeze-weed, H.	Composite.	Yellow.	Conn. to Minn., south and west.	River banks, wet grounds.	Sept.	
*Snowberry, Creeping (see Creeping Snowberry).						

SPECIES AND VARIETIES.	Family.	Color.	Locality.	Environment.	Time of bloom.	Pages.
Snowdrop, G.	Amaryllis.	White.	From Europe, gardens.	Grassy ground.	Mar., Apr.	3, 108
Snow on the Mountain, E	Spurge.	White, tip leaves white.	Minn. to Mo. W. to Col., E. to Ohio, and gardens.	Plains.	Aug., Sept.	209
Soapwort (see Bouncing Bet)						187
*Solanum Carolinense (see Horse-nettle).						242
Solanum Dulcamara (see Nightshade)						244
*Solanum Nigrum (see Nightshade, Common).						
Solanum Pseudo-Capsicum (see Jerusalem Cherry).						244
*Solanum Torreyi.	Night-shade.	Light violet.	E. Kan. and Tex.	Prairies.	June-Aug.	
Solanum tuberosum.						244
Solidago altissima, G	Composite.	Bright yellow.	Common.	Fields and copses.	Aug., Sept.	217
Solidago arguta.	Composite.	Greenish-yellow.	N. H. to Pa., and N. E. Minn.	Moist copses and woods.	July-Sept.	217
Solidago bicolor.	Composite.	Cream-white.	N. E., W. to Minn. and Mo.	Roadsides and copses.	Aug.-Oct.	221
Solidago cæsia.	Composite.	Bright yellow.	N. E., W. to Minn., Ill., and Ky.	Moist and shady thickets.	Aug.-Nov.	222
Solidago Canadensis.	Composite.	Deep yellow.	Common.	Borders of field and thickets.	Aug.-Oct.	218
Solidago lanceolata.	Composite.	Greenish-yellow.	Common.	River banks and moist soil.	Aug.-Oct.	219
Solidago latifolia.	Composite.	Bright yellow.	Common, northward, S. along mts.	Moist, shaded banks.	Aug., Sept.	222

A SYSTEMATICAL INDEX.

Solidago nemoralis	......	Composite.	Rich golden yellow.	Common.	Pastures, sterile fields.	Early Aug.	218
Solidago odora	......	Composite.	Greenish-yellow.	Me. and Vt. to Ky., and southward.	Sandy soil, by thickets.	Aug., Sept.	222
Solidago rugosa	......	Composite.	Greenish-yellow.	Common.	Borders of fields, copses.	Late July-Sept.	218
Solidago sempervirens	......	Composite.	Deep yellow.	Me. to Va.	Salt marshes, and by rocks.	Aug.-Oct.	221
Solidago speciosa	......	Composite.	Bright golden yellow.	Me. to Minn., and southward.	Copses.	Aug., Sept.	223
Solidago tenuifolia	......	Composite.	Greenish-yellow.	Mass. to Ill. and southward.	Sandy places near the coast.	Aug.-Oct.	219
Solidago ulmifolia	......	Composite.	Yellow.	Common.	Low copses.	Aug., Sept.	217
Solomon's Seal, P.	......	Lily.	Cream-white.	N. E. to Fla., W. to Minn., E. Kan., and Tex.	Wooded banks.	May, June.	36
Solomon's Seal, False (see False Solomon's Seal)							37, 199
Spanish Bayonet (see *Yucca aloifolia*)							
*Spatter-Dock (see Pond-Lily, Yellow).							
Spiderwort, T.	......	Mayaca.	Blue-violet.	N. Y. to Fla., W. to Minn., Tex., and Rocky Mts.	Rich ground.	June, July.	100, 101
*Spikenard, A.	......	Dogwood.	Greenish-white.	N. E. to Minn., S. to mts. of Ga.	Rich woodlands.	July.	37, 95
Spiræa Japonica	......						168
Spiræa salicifolia (see Meadow-sweet)							169
Spiræa tomentosa (see Hardhack)							
Spiranthes cernua, L.	......	Orchis.	White.	E. and S., common.	Wet places.	Sept., Oct.	214
Spiranthes gracilis	......	Orchis.	Cream-white.	Common.	Hilly woods and sandy plains.	July-Oct.	214

Species and Varieties.	Family.	Color.	Locality.	Environment.	Time of bloom.	Pages.
Spreading Dogbane (see Dogbane).						
Spring Beauty, C.	Purslane.	Pale pink.	Common West and South.	Moist, open woods.	Apr., May.	160
*Stachys Betonica (see Betony).						18
Squill (see Scilla).						4
Stagger-Bush, A.	Heath.	Pinky-white.	R. I. to Fla., Tenn., and Ark.	Low grounds.	May, June.	84
Star-Flower, T.	Primrose.	White.	N. E. to Minn., S. to N. Ind. and mts. of Va.	Damp, cold woods.	May.	23, 157
Star-Grass, Yellow (see Yellow Star-Grass)						50, 108
Star of Bethlehem, O.	Lily.	White.	Scarcely common, gardens.	Low meadows.	June.	101
Starry Campion (see Campion, Starry)						129
Starwort (see Aster)						226
Starwort, Northern (see Stellaria borealis)						131
*Statice Caroliniana (see Sea-Lavender).						
Steeple-bush (see Hardhack)						169, 183
Stellaria borealis, S	Pink.	White.	R. I. to Minn., and northward.	Shaded or wet places.	June-Aug.	131
Stellaria longifolia, S.	Pink.	White.	Common, northward.	Grassy places.	June, July.	131
Stellaria media (see Common Chickweed)						131
Stitchwort, Long-leaved (see Stellaria longifolia).						131
Strawberry, Wild, F.	Rose.	White.	Common.	Rich woodlands and fields.	May-July.	52
Strawberry, Yellow-flowered, F.	Rose.	Yellow.	From India, Staten Island, Phila., and southward.	Fields.	May-Aug.	51
*Streptopus amplexifolius (see Twisted-stalk).						153
Summer Chrysanthemum (see Chrysanthemum, Summer).						

A SYSTEMATICAL INDEX.

Name	Family	Color	Range	Soil	Time	Page
*Sundew, Round-leaved, D	Sundew.	White.	N. E. to Minn., Ind. and southward, common.	Peat bogs.	July, Aug.	
*Sundew, Thread-leaved, D	Sundew.	Pale magenta.	Mass. to N. J. and Fla.	Wet sand near coast.	July, Aug.	
Sundrops, O	Evening-Primrose.	Yellow.	N. E. to N. J., W. to Minn. and Kan.	Dry fields.	June.	76
Sunflower, Garden, H	Composite.	Golden yellow.	Minn. to Tex. and W., and gardens.	Light, rich soil.	Aug., Sept.	208
Sunflower, Globosus fistulosus	Composite.	All bright golden yellow.	Minn. to Tex., gardens.		Aug.-Oct.	208
Sunflower, Maximilian's, H				Prairies.		209
Sunflower, Oscar Wilde						208
Sunflower, Primrose	Composite.	Deep golden yellow.	Gardens.	Light soil.	Aug., Sept.	209
Sunflower, Sutton's Miniature, H						180, 208
Sunflower, Wild, H	Composite.	Light golden yellow.	Common.	Low thickets and swamps.	Aug., Sept.	178, 186
*Swan River Daisy, B	Composite.	Purple center, violet-blue.	From Australia, gardens.	Light soil.	July, Aug.	
Sweet Alyssum, A	Mustard.	White.	Gardens.	Light soil.	June-Aug.	89, 172
*Sweet Cicely, O	Parsley.	White.	N. E. to Va., W. to Tenn., E. Kan., and Dak.	Rich, moist woods.	May, June.	
Sweet Flag, A	Arum.	Yellowish-green.	N. E. to Fla., W. to Minn., Iowa, and E. Kan.	Stream margins and swamps.	June.	74
Sweet Pea, L	Pulse.	Various.	From Europe, gardens.	Rich, clayey soil.	June-Oct.	114, 204
Sweet Sultan, C	Composite.	Yellow, pink, and purple.	From Asia, gardens.	Light soil.	July-Sept.	91
Symplocarpus fœtidus (see Skunk Cabbage)						5

300 FAMILIAR FLOWERS OF FIELD AND GARDEN.

SPECIES AND VARIETIES.	Family.	Color.	Locality.	Environment.	Time of bloom.	Pages.
Tagetes erecta (see Marigold, African)						203
Tagetes patula (see Marigold, French)						203
Tagetes signata	Composite.	Claret-spotted, yellow.	From Mexico and South America, gardens.			203
Tanacetum vulgare (see Tansy).						180
Tansy, T.	Composite.	Deep yellow.	Atlantic States, common.	Light soil.	July–Sept.	142, 180, 183
Taraxacum Dens-leonis or *officinale* (see Dandelion, Common).						103
*Tear Thumb, P.	Buckwheat.	White or flesh-color.	From Asia, common.	Low grounds.	June–Oct.	
Teasel, Wild, D.	Teasel.	Lilac.	Common.	Along roads.	Aug., Sept.	208
Thalictrum anemonoides (see Rue Anemone).					June–Aug.	17
Thalictrum Cornuti or *polygamum* (see Meadow Rue, Tall).						18, 158
Thalictrum dioicum (see Meadow-Rue, Early).						
*Thistle, Common, C.	Composite.	Purple.	Common, northward.	Pastures and roadsides.	June–Aug.	159
Thorn-Apple, D.	Nightshade.	White.	Common.	Waste grounds.	Aug., Sept.	150, 183
Thoroughwort (see Boneset).						
Tiarella cordifolia, F.	Saxifrage.	White.	N. E. to Minn. and Ind., S. in the mts.	Rich, moist woods.	Apr., May.	213
Tiger-Flower (see *Tigridia Pavonia*).						25
Tigridia Pavonia, T.	Iris.	Scarlet and yellow.	From Mexico, gardens.	Light soil.	July–Sept.	198
Toadflax, Wild Blue, L.	Figwort.	Pale bluepurple.	Common.	Sandy soil.	June–Aug.	198, 202
Toadflax, Yellow, L.	Figwort.	Yellow and orange.	From Europe, common.	Fields and roadsides.	July–Oct.	174
Tobacco, Common, N.	Nightshade.	Pink-red.	Cultivated for foliage, also gardens.	Light soil.	June–Sept.	142, 173, 183
						188, 190

Tobacco, White-flowered, N.	Night-shade.			Light soil.	June–Sept.	76, 190
*Toothwort (see Crinkle-Root).						
Touch-me-not (see Jewel-weed).						171
Tradescantia Virginica (see Spiderwort).						100, 101
Trailing Arbutus (see Arbutus).						1
Trichostema dichotomum (see Blue-Curls).						23
Trientalis Americana (see Star-Flower).						22
Trillium erectum, B.	Lily.	Dull red-brown.	N. E. to N. C., W. to Minn. and Mo.	Rich woods.	Apr., May.	21
Trillium erythrocarpum (see Trillium, Painted).						20
Trillium grandiflorum, T.	Lily.	White.	N. E. to N. C., W. to Minn. and Mo.	Rich woods.	Apr., May.	20
Trillium, Large White (see *Trillium grandiflorum*).						
Trillium, Painted, T.	Lily.	White, crimson marks.	N. E. to Ga., W. to Wis. and Mo.	Cold, damp woods and bogs.	Apr., May.	21
Tritoma Uvaria, K. R.	Lily.	Light scarlet and yellow.	From Cape of Good Hope, gardens.	Light soil.	Aug.–Oct.	199
Tropæolum majus (see Nasturtium).						111
Tropæolum peregrinum (see Canary-Bird Flower).						115
Tuberose, P.	Amaryllis.	White.	From Mexico, gardens.	Rich, light soil.	Sept.	107, 202
Tulip, T.	Lily.	Various.	From Asia Minor, gardens.	Good soil.	May, June.	11, 199
Tulip, Bleu Celeste.						12
Tulipa Gesneriana (see Tulip).						11
Turtle-head, C.	Figwort.	Crimson-pink tinge, white.	N. E. to Minn., S. to Fla. and Tex.	Wet places.	July–Sept.	157
*Twin-Flower, L.	Honey-suckle.	Purple-white.	N. E. to N. J, and mts. of Md., W. to Minn.	Mossy woods and cold bogs.	June.	

302 FAMILIAR FLOWERS OF FIELD AND GARDEN.

SPECIES AND VARIETIES.	Family.	Color.	Locality.	Environment.	Time of bloom.	Pages.
*Twisted-Stalk, S.	Lily.	Greenish cream-white.	N.E. to N. Minn., S. to Ohio, Pa., mts. to N.C.	Cold, moist woods.	June.	
*Typha latifolia (see Cat-tail Flag).						
*Utricularia purpurea	Bladder-wort.	Violet-purple.	Me., N. Pa. to Fla., Lake Co., Ind.	Ponds near coast.	June-Aug.	
*Utricularia vulgaris (see Bladderwort).						
Uvularia perfoliata	Lily.	Cream-yellow.	N. E. to Dak., and southward.	Rich woods.	Apr., May.	16
Vaccinium macrocarpon (see Cranberry)						
*Velvet Flower (see Salpiglossis sinuata).						
Veratrum viride (see Indian Poke).						63
Verbascum Thapsus (see Mullein).						79
Verbena Aubletia						182
						131
*Verbena chamaedrifolia	Vervain.	Lilac and purple.	Ind. and Ill. to Fla., Ark., and N. Mex.	Open woods and prairies.	June-Aug.	
Verbena hastata (see Vervain)	Vervain.	Scarlet.	From S. America, gardens.	Light soil.	June-Aug.	
*Verbena pulchella						132
Verbena teucroides	Vervain.	Magenta.	From S. America, gardens.	Light soil.	June-Aug.	
	Vervain.	Pink.	From S. America, gardens.	Light soil.	June-Aug.	131
Vernonia Noveboracensis (see Iron-weed)						234
*Veronica Americana (see Brookline, American).						
Vervain, Blue	Vervain.	Violet.	Common.	Waste grounds and roadsides.	July, Aug.	132
*Vetch, Common, V	Pulse.	Violet-purple.	N.E. to N.J. and S.W. to Mich. and Minn.	Fields and waste places.	June-Aug.	

A SYSTEMATICAL INDEX.

Viburnum lantanoides (see Hobble-Bush)					80
Vicia sativa (see Vetch).					
**Vinca minor* (see Periwinkle).					35
Viola blanda (see Sweet White V.).					23, 32
**Viola canina* (see Dog V.).					
Viola cucullata (see Purple V.).					11
**Viola lanceolata* (see Lance-leaved V.).					
Viola odorata (see Sweet English V.).					33
**Viola palustris* (see Marsh V.).					31
Viola pedata (see Bird-foot V.).					10
Viola pubescens (see Downy Yellow V.).					33
Viola tricolor (see Pansy).					
Violet, Bird-foot, V.	Violet.	Purple.	N. E. to Minn., and southward.	Sandy soil.	May.	33
Violet, Bird-foot, var. bicolor.	Violet.	Light and dark purple.	Mass. to Md.	Shale.	May.	
*Violet, Dog	Violet.	Light purple.	Common.	Low grounds.	May–July.	9
Violet, Dog's-Tooth (see Adder's Tongue)					31
Violet, Downy Yellow	Violet.	Light yellow.	Common.	Rich woods.	May.	
*Violet, Lance-leaved	Violet.	White, purple veins.	Common, eastward.	Damp soil.	May.	
*Violet, Marsh	Violet.	Light lilac, purple streaks.	Alpine summits of White Mountains.	Cold, wet grounds.	June.	
Violet, Purple or Blue	Violet.	Purple.	Common.	Low grounds.	May.	23, 32
Violet, Sweet English	Violet.	Purple.	From England and Italy, gardens.	Shady grounds.	May.	11, 107
Violet, Sweet White	Violet.	White, purple veins.	Common.	Rich woods.	May.	35
Viper's Bugloss, E.	Borage.	Reddish-purple to violet-blue.	From Europe, Middle Atlantic States.	Roadsides and meadows.	June–Sept.	142, 195

304 FAMILIAR FLOWERS OF FIELD AND GARDEN.

SPECIES AND VARIETIES.	Family.	Color.	Locality.	Environment.	Time of bloom.	Pages.
Virginia-Creeper, A	Vine.	Greenish.	Common.	Low or rich ground.	July.	138
Virgin's-Bower (see *Clematis Virginiana*)						138
Wake Robin (see *Trillium erectum*)						22
Water Arum, C	Arum.	White.	N. E. to N. J., W. to Mich. and Minn. and northward.	Cold bogs.	June.	132
Water-cress, N	Mustard.	White.	From Europe, common.	Brooks and streamlets.	June, July.	115
Water-Lily, White, N	Water-lily.	White.	Common.	Ponds, still water.	June–Sept.	185
*Water Plantain, A	Water-Plantain.	Sometimes pale pink-white.	Common.	Shallow water and ditches.	Aug., Sept.	
*Western Daisy (see Daisy, Western).						
Whiteweed (see Daisy, Ox-eye)						
*Whitlavia grandiflora, P	Waterleaf.	Violet-purple.	California and gardens.	Good soil.	July, Aug.	105
*Whitlow-Grass, D	Mustard.	White.	Common.	Sandy, waste places.	Apr., May.	
Wild Carrot (see Carrot).						95
*Wild Ginger, Canada, A	Birthwort.	Brownish-purple.	Common north.	On hillsides, in rich woods.	Apr., May.	
Wild Hyacinth, C-S	Lily.	Pale violet-blue.	W. Pa. to Minn. and E. Kan., mts. Ga.	Rich ground.	Apr., May.	5
*Wild Indigo (see Indigo, Wild).						
Wild Meadow Parsnip (see Parsnip).						96
Wild Mustard (see Mustard)						83
*Wild Pink (see *Silene Pennsylvanica*).						
*Wild Sarsaparilla (see Sarsaparilla, Wild).						133
Wild Teasel (see Teasel)						208

Name	Family	Color	Range	Habitat	Time	Page
Willow-Herb, Great (see Fireweed).						210
Willow, Swamp.						212
Wind-flower (see Anemone, Wood).						16
Winterberry (see Black Alder).						244
Winterberry, Smooth, I						244
	Holly.	White.	Me. to mts. of Va.	Wet grounds.	June.	
*Winter-Cress, B	Mustard.	Yellow.	Lake Superior, northward and westward, and old gardens.	Rich soil.	May-July.	29
Wintergreen, Aromatic, G	Heath.	Waxy white.	Me. to Minn., S. to N. Ga., and far northward.	Cool, damp woods.	July.	137, 138
Witch-Hazel, H	Witch-hazel.	Yellow.	N. E. to Fla., W. to E. Minn. and La.	Damp woods.	Oct.	16
Wood Anemone (see Anemone, Wood).						
*Wood Betony, P	Figwort.	Green-yellow and purplish.	Common.	Copses and banks.	May-July.	
*Wood-Sorrel, Violet, O	Geranium.	Violet.	Most common southward.	Rocky places and open woods.	May, June.	
Wood-Sorrel, White, O	Geranium.	White, crimson lines.	N. E. to Pa. Lake Superior, and north, S. in Alleghanies.	Deep, cold woods.	June, July.	71, 119
Wood-Sorrel, Yellow, O	Geranium.	Yellow.	Common.	Waste ground and roadsides.	May-Oct.	71
*Xyris flexuosa (see Yellow-eyed Grass).						
Yarrow, Common, A.	Composite.	Gray-white some pink.	Common.	Fields, hills, roadsides.	July-Oct.	175
*Yellow-eyed Grass, X.	Yellow-eyed grass.	Yellow.	Mass. to Fla., W. to Minn. and Mo.	Sandy bogs.	June-Aug.	

SPECIES AND VARIETIES.	Family.	Color.	Locality.	Environment.	Time of bloom.	Pages.
*Yellow Pond-Lily (see Pond-Lily).						
Yellow Star-Grass, H.	Amaryllis.	Yellow.	N. E. to Fla., W. to Minn., Tex., E. Kan.	Meadows and open woods.	May, June.	50, 108
Yucca aloifolia	Lily.	Cream-white.	N. C., southward, gardens.	Sandy soil, near coast.	July.	199
Yucca angustifolia	Lily.	Cream-white.	S. Dak. to Iowa, Kan. and N. Mex. and gardens.	Light, sandy soil.	May, June.	199
Yucca filamentosa	Lily.	Cream-white or purplish.	Md. to Fla. and La., and gardens.	Sandy soil, near coast.	July.	199, 202
Yucca gloriosa	Lily.	Tinged purple, cream-white.	N. C., southward, gardens.	Sandy soil, near coast.	June–July.	199
Zephyranthes Atamasco (see Atamasco Lily)						107
Zephyr Flower (see Zephyranthes Atamasco)						107
Zinnia, Crested						206
Zinnia elegans	Composite.	Various colors.	From Mexico, gardens.	Light soil.	June–Sept.	202, 205
Zinnia Jacqueminot						206
Zizia aurea (see Parsnip, Wild Meadow)						96

INDEX FOR LOCALITIES.

Africa, 14.
Alleghany Mountains, 61, 196.
Argentine Republic, 131.
Arkansas, 201.
Asia, 91.
Asia Minor, 11, 147.

Bergen Park, Col., 130.
Berkshire, 138, 169.
Boston, 3, 6, 29, 108, 138, 157, 195, 240, 242, 246.
Brooklyn, 19, 25, 159.
Buzzard's Bay, 35.

California, 148, 189, 199.
Campton, N. H., 22, 25, 48, 54, 76, 79, 83, 88, 156, 158, 216, 224, 227.
Cape Cod, Mass., 63, 126, 164.
Cape of Good Hope, 116, 197, 199.
Carolinas, 108, 131, 153, 193.
Catskill Mountains, 99, 157, 168.
Central Park, 54.
Chili, 106, 111.
China, 190, 232, 246.
Clarendon Hills, Mass., 242.
Cologne, 216.
Concord, Mass., 133.
Constantinople, 12.
Crawford Notch, White Mountains, 30, 165.

Eastern States, 9, 23, 61, 100.
England, 3, 11, 12, 105, 141, 246.
Esopus Creek, N. Y., 195.

Europe, 12, 89, 90, 142, 190, 195, 197, 202, 238, 243.

Florida, 100, 194.
France, 74, 106, 107, 152, 197, 246.
Franconia Mountains, 12.
Franconia Notch, 71.

Germany, 90.
Gibraltar, 89, 92.
Greenland, 98, 145.

Haarlem, Holland, 11.
Hastings-on-the-Hudson, 83.
Himalayas, 63.
Hoboken, 195.
Holland, 11, 12.
Hudson, Valley of the, 157, 195.

Illinois, 131.
India, 116, 121, 147, 149.
Indian Territory, 194.
Italy, 8, 11, 91, 141.

Japan, 97, 105, 140, 232, 246.

Kansas, 104, 242.

Lake George, 169.
Lakewood, N. J., 108.
Levant, The, 91, 197, 200.
Long Island, N. Y., 19, 85, 240.
Louisiana, 152.

Maine, 63, 221, 223.
Maryland, 104, 242.
Massachusetts, 2, 3, 29, 61, 108.
Mexico, 49, 121, 198, 199, 202, 203, 206, 210, 246.
Missouri, 153.
Montpelier, 210.
Morristown, N. J., 102.
Mount Washington, 10, 97, 131, 165.

Nantucket, Mass., 25, 63, 104.
Neponset River, 195.
New England, 1, 2, 3, 82, 86, 96, 98, 117, 123, 126, 134, 153, 164, 194, 210, 212, 228, 245.
New Hampshire, 19, 26, 61, 70, 83, 84, 88, 102, 131, 138, 160, 195, 208, 230, 245.
New Jersey, 19, 53, 63, 70, 85, 86, 108, 121, 138, 160, 168, 196, 209, 223, 230, 235.
New York, 19, 53, 96, 100, 101, 105, 117, 160, 199, 234, 246.

Ohio, 5.

Palestine, 89.
Pemigewasset River, 40, 136.
Pemigewasset Valley, 12, 31, 53, 85, 211, 240, 242, 243.
Pennsylvania, 86, 132, 141, 191, 195, 238.
Persia, 12, 147.
Peru, 106, 111.
Philadelphia, 53.

Prospect Park, Brooklyn, 2, 19, 102.
Public Garden, Boston, 5, 62.
Pyrenees Mountains, 238.

Rome, 141.
Roxbury, Mass., 4.

Saddle River, N. J., 70.
Scotland, 141, 165.
Siberia, 5, 190.
Silver Lake, Staten Island, 45.
South America, 111, 120, 131, 135, 203.
Spain, 89.
Squam Lake, N. H., 85.
St. Bernard Pass, 108.
Staten Island, 10, 51.
Switzerland, 108.
Syria, 192.

Texas, 92, 104, 153, 202, 208, 242, 246.
Thibet, 139.

United States, 193.

Vermont, 27.
Virginia, 195, 196, 221.

Waterville, N. H., 80.
Wells River, Vt., 210.
White Hills (the White Mountains), 2, 40, 83, 136, 156, 169, 242.
White Mountains, 2, 16, 25, 28, 29, 32, 35, 52, 62, 64, 65, 67, 70, 71, 80, 88, 156, 221, 238, 245.

THE END.